TRAVELS
with JJ

Lori Stewart

D1569647

A Travelogue

One Woman's Fanciful Musings During a Drive
Across America with Her Dogs, Jenny & Jeff

TRAVELS *with* JJ

Lon Stewart

Also by Lori Stewart

If I had as many grandchildren as you...
Grandma Aren't You Glad the World's
Finally in Color Today?

TRAVELS *with* JJ

Lori Stewart

A Travelogue

One Woman's Fanciful Musings During a Drive
Across America with Her Dogs, Jenny & Jeff

Palmar Press

Layout & Cover Design: Chad B. Freeman
Cover Photo: Philip Geiger

Published in the United States of America by Palmar Press.
First Edition, 2018

Publisher's Cataloging-in-Publication data
(Prepared by the Donohue Group)

Stewart, Lori Scott.
Travels with JJ (Jenny and Jeff)

SUMMARY:
One woman's fanciful musings during a drive across America with her dogs, Jenny
and Jeff

ISBN-13: 978-0-9839293-2-1 (softcover)

1. Travel 2. Traveler's writing America 3. Animals - Dogs 4. Memoir

For Mom,
With special thanks to Monterey Bay Lab Rescue for
Jenny and Jeff (JJ), and all the big-hearted and generous
friends and family across the country who hosted us on
these cross-country travels.

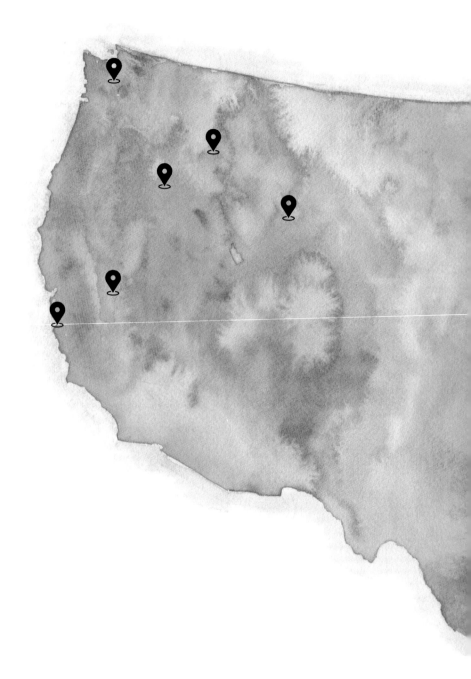

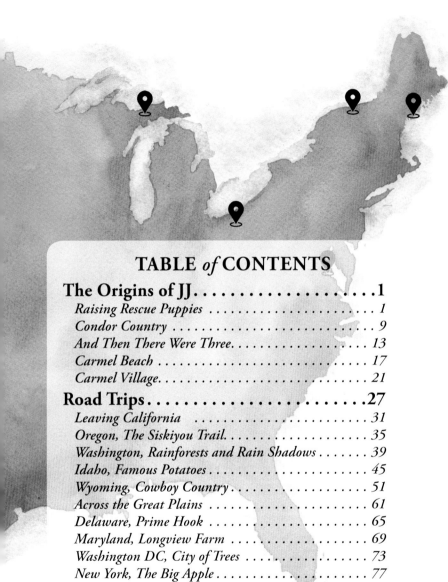

TABLE *of* CONTENTS

Dog, n.

A kind of additional or subsidiary Deity designed to catch the overflow and surplus of the world's worship.

Ambrose Bierce

The Origins of JJ
Raising Rescue Puppies

We never really knew the whole story. This is what we were told: the owners of a pregnant golden retriever and black lab father went on a vacation cruise, and left a dog-sitter in charge. Best laid plans not only go awry, sometimes they alter tragically. The golden retriever mother died suddenly after giving birth to her five golden-lab mix puppies.

Newborn puppies, like all newborns, require a great deal of mothering—warmth, stimulation and round-the-clock feeding. The sitter did her best to care for the puppies, but was soon completely overwhelmed. So she called Monterey Bay Lab Rescue, and Lab Rescue called me. And I did what any self-respecting daughter would do, I called Mom.

Mom was in her eighties and had just come home from the hospital, having been told she had only a few weeks to live.

"Mom," I said. "You're not going to die. There's nothing wrong with you that hasn't always been wrong with you, and we could save these newborns. I can't do it alone. Will you help?"

Well, Mom did what I knew she'd do. She got up, got dressed, combed her still brown wavy hair, put on her apple blossom red lipstick, and off we went to meet the puppies. It just happened to be her birthday.

These newborn retriever puppies looked rather like sea otters, with flat furry muzzles, closed eyes, tiny ears on the sides of their heads, tiny otter tails, and legs that didn't yet work. Unable to crawl, they squirmed and squeaked and scooted around on their bellies in an endless search for milk and the warmth of their littermates.

Our orphan puppies, three golden and two black, came in a cardboard box with a heating pad in the bottom, and

in the corner, a soft brown stuffed dog outfitted with a ticking, throbbing heart. The puppies loved this cuddly surrogate and snuggled beneath her as though she were real.

The ingenious faux mom was designed in such a way that, in theory, we could put tiny bottles of milk in her stomach, push the nipples through holes in her stuffed belly, and the puppies could nurse naturally. In practice, hungry over-eager puppies ended up pushing the nipples back through the hole and whining woefully about their lost food source. It was an interesting experiment. But in the end, we found it best just to bottle-feed them by hand.

Every two hours on the dot, the puppies would start squirming and squeaking like baby kittens. Mom and I would then fill their preemie baby bottles with a formula of warm goat's milk and Similac and feed them carefully, keeping them upright to make sure they sucked properly so the milk would go into their stomachs and not their lungs. And then we'd stimulate them.

Newborn puppies are unable to eliminate on their own, so the mother dog licks their little bottoms to activate their digestive systems. This part of mothering is crucial for their survival. So, after each feeding we'd wipe their tiny bums with wet cotton pads, and wait for success.

This went on for four weeks. We'd feed one puppy, stimulate it, put it in a warm robe pocket and move on to feed the next one. By the time we completed this routine with all the puppies, it was time to start over—rather like painting the Golden Gate Bridge. Feeding orphan puppies quickly

Jenny, Jeff, Jack, Jonathon, Jiminy – Photos by: Miranda Wheeler became a community effort, and friends and neighbors stopped by all hours of the day to help. The community was less enthusiastic about the follow-up stimulation duties.

We gave all the puppies names beginning with the letter J, thinking they would be easier to remember. And so they became Jenny, Jeffrey, Jack, Jonathon and Jiminy, the runt of the litter. A neighbor noted that J was originally a swash letter, a typographical flourish for the letter I, and that in its original form, it looked rather like the tail of a subdued dog. He wondered if that was why I gave them J names. I can honestly say, no—swash letter flourishes never crossed my mind.

Despite what taxonomists might say, I am convinced that golden retriever puppies and sea otters are closely related—at least in appearance and behavior if not classification. They both have big eyes and whiskered snouts and inquisitive, playful personalities. They race and wrestle and somersault, nip at each other's paws, and nose each other into action.

I'm also convinced that at some point in their evolution, golden retriever puppies were related to birds. When the Js were about four weeks old and ready for solid food, they began bobbing their heads up and down and opening their mouths, as though waiting for us to deposit food into their muzzles, the way mother birds do. I am no mother bird, but I knew what they wanted, so I'd head to the stove, warm up a mixture of vegetables, meat, canned pumpkin and milk and take it into the yard to feed them three times a day— breakfast, lunch and dinner.

They loved these meals, nearly as much as the baby blue jays that perched on the patio chairs, waiting for them to finish. When they first began to eat solid food, they would jump into their bowls and splash the food all over the patio— great leavings for the blue jays. But Jenny figured it out and taught the boys not to play with their food, or she would have to eat it… *as a service…* just to keep the jays at bay.

The Puppy Nanny

When the puppies were about four weeks old, a family friend— young artist, photographer, musician and animal lover—arrived for a visit. She stretched out on the floor, and immediately, they crawled onto her face and snuggled under her neck. She became the Puppy Nanny.

By this time, the puppies had distinct personalities, so the Puppy Nanny immediately gave them proper names and nicknames. Jenny, a golden girl with a tiny splash of white on her nose was Jennifer Allison McKnight Stewart, aka *the Instigator*. Jeffrey, Jenny's golden twin brother was named Robinson Jeffers Samwise Stewart, aka *Mama's Boy* or alternatively Swiper. Jack, who takes after his dad and is a larger black version of Jeffrey, was named Jackson Maxwell Stewart Leavitt, aka *Blackjack*. Jonathon, a golden lab was Jonathon Steinbeck Stewart, aka *Bear*; and Jiminy, a little black lab with a patch of white like Jenny's was the runt of the litter and appropriately named Jiminy Cricket Stewart, aka *Yoda*.

The boys were mellow. Jenny was not. In fact, she came out of the womb rather frantic, as though worried everyone was getting more milk than she. She was a bit bossy— constantly pouncing on the others, nudging them into a game of chase.

Chase was a running game played on our indoor/outdoor track, which wound from the dog door in the back bedroom, across the yard, through the dog door in the kitchen, and then into the living room, dining room and hallway and back to the bedrooms. After about five rounds on the track, Jack would charge through the back dog door, turn around half-in and half-out and hold the fort, thus changing the direction of the chase. Eventually they'd run out of steam. I'd call them over and they'd collapsed into a giant puppy pile on the red plaid dog bed that became known as "the circle of trust."

Mom enjoyed watching this game immensely. She would sit in her favorite chair in the dining room with the sun on her back, and beam as the puppies raced past her round and round. I began to see watching puppy play as a potent life force, almost as potent as being needed. Mom defied the doctors' prognosis and would continue to get up, dress, do her hair and put on her lipstick for another year and a half.

Our house became a puppy palace. The tiled entryway, with walls of paned glass windows was light and bright, and the perfect day room for the puppies. We furnished it with plenty of warm blankets and towels, and made tunnels and climbing platforms.

The *Js* would root around playing for an hour or so and then sleep. Once they were fast asleep, the Puppy Nanny, who had turned the living room into a photography studio, would pick them up one at a time, and carefully arrange them into letters—a puppy alphabet as it were, because you never know when you're going to need an original font. Talk about your typographical flourishes.

House training was fairly easy, since puppies won't foul their own space if they can help it. The minute they'd awaken, we would simply open the front door and let them out on the walkway to do their business. Obedience training was bit trickier because they were so bonded—little musketeers

Puppy Letters – Photos by: Miranda Wheeler

Big Sur – Photo by: Sam Farr

subscribing full on to—"one for all and all for one." They were easily distracted if they were together, and separating them for individual training sessions just made all the puppies cry.

In order to begin our travels, all I really needed them to do was follow me as a group. Lacking a flute, I put pennies in a jar, which I jangled while mincing down the garden pathway. They learned to follow me everywhere, like proper little ducklings. The pennies-in-a-jar prompt was not foolproof, but certainly good enough for our first trip—an outing to Big Sur.

Big Sur Cattle – Photo by: Don Graham CC SA 2.0

Condor Country

El Sur Grande, The Big South, Big Sur—that's where we were headed—into that legendary expanse of untrammeled scenic wilderness that stretches for ninety miles along the California coast from Carmel south to San Simeon. For years, the ranchos and homesteads of the region were accessible only by horse and ship. Finally in 1937 Cabrillo Highway, Highway 1, California's First Scenic Highway, was completed, giving poets, writers, photographers, puppies and people like us access to the area.

We packed the *J Team* into a warm, well-padded crate and headed down the coast, along the ocean-side lane of the road, clinging to the rocky cliffs that fall precipitously into the Pacific Ocean on our right, and rise abruptly up into the Santa Lucia Mountains on our left. For those afraid of heights, I suggest you drive north from San Simeon, where you will be on the inside lane.

We stopped briefly at Point Lobos, that spectacular "meeting of land and sea" discovered by the Spanish, who thought the sea lions they heard barking were wolves—hence the name Punta de los Lobos Marinos, or Point of the Sea Wolves. We continued south across the iconic Bixby Bridge, and headed into the rolling green pasture-lands overlooking Pt. Sur.

In my next life, if I *must* come back as a cow, I would like to live right there on El Sur Ranch. The grass is green and lush and garnished with poppies and lupine. The water running into the ocean from the Little Sur River is spring fresh and icy cold. And the views in every direction are stunning. I could stand out in that field for years watching for shipwrecks and migrating whales. I would see sunrays streaming through storm clouds and reflecting off late afternoon fog that sifts in and out of coastal canyons, and waterfalls, and rising moons, and star trails, blowholes and backlit arches that dot the coastal beaches below. And I would bask in the shadow of Pico Blanco, a sacred place from where Native Rumsien and Esselen people believed all life originated.

The Puppy Nanny captured it all with the camera that was attached to her back like a camel hump. We drove on past rustic artist colonies, and lavish secluded hideaways with colorful pasts and spectacular views and infinity pools that appear to flow over the edge of the mountain to the blue Pacific a thousand feet below.

We continued on past Henry Miller Memorial Library, "the place where nothing happens (except on occasion)"— *nothings* like composer Phillip Glass' concert outside among the redwoods, where a handful of people gathered spellbound as they watched his fingers float over the piano keys and wondered if the people racing up and down the coast highway had any idea what was going on there.

Finally, 16 points down the road, we arrived at our destination. We pulled the crate out of the car, opened the gate and let the puppies run wild on the thick lush green grass. Actually, the puppies crawled out, ran in a circle and collapsed in our laps. Apparently, travel was quite exhausting.

After hours of photo taking, we gathered them into a wheelbarrow and rolled them to the upper grassy area to enjoy the ocean views and listen to some music, which the Puppy Nanny produced by pulling a guitar out of her second camel hump. There must be something about music that touches animals, because the puppies were drawn to it. They crawled into her lap as she played and put their ears on the back of the guitar—as if to feel close to the vibrations, to the harmony.

After the concert, we all tumbled and rolled down the hills, frolicked and played chase until a shadow passed over us. When I looked up, I saw a VERY... VERY large bird circling overhead. And that's when it occurred to me that… *we were in condor country.*

Jeffrey in Big Sur – Photo by: Miranda Wheeler

Condors with their 10-foot wingspan are the largest flying land birds in the western hemisphere, and by the early 1980's they were nearly extinct. In 1987, the Ventana Wildlife Society captured all known wild condors and initiated a successful captive breeding program. Their numbers rose, and in 1991, the Society reintroduced condors into the wild. These majestic birds can now be seen flying over the mountains and valleys, and it seemed this might be one of them. This was terribly exciting until I realized that a condor might not be able to distinguish between an adorable golden retriever lab-mix-sleeping-puppy and a dead rodent. And maybe it wasn't a condor, could be an eagle, but whatever it was, it seemed to have its eyes on *us*.

We scrambled about and herded the puppies into the crate; covered it with a warm blanket and put it in the back of the car—away from giant condors and anything else that could be after them. The J's fell fast asleep in a pile, and we headed back up the coast—on the inside lane.

It was a perfect day in a perfect place. The bright blue sky was cloudless and crystal clear. As the sun started to set, the endless expanse of ocean seemed lit from within, emitting a kind of silvery light. For expert ocean watchers, these conditions foreshadow the illusive *green flash*—that optical phenomenon that occurs on a clear day when the yellow sun melts into the blue water and creates a spark of green. We pulled off the road to watch the setting sun, and the Puppy Nanny captured it on film. The puppies slept on, their tiny legs spinning as they dreamed of their first away day in the wilds of Big Sur.

Double Rainbow Carmel Beach – Photo by: Judy Kreger, Monterey Bay Lab Rescue

And Then There Were Three

We tried not to become too attached to these puppies, since we knew that even though they had made it this far, there was still only a slim chance they'd survive. Without the nutrients and antibodies in mother's milk, our puppies' immune systems were badly compromised. If they got sick, there'd be no way to know what was wrong or how to cure them. Blood work shows nothing, and the five-week old puppies were simply too young to treat with medications or vaccines.

Jonathon, Jeffrey and Jiminy did get sick. They started to fade, and within two days, Jonathon and Jiminy had died. The vet decided to take extraordinary measures with Jeffrey. He gave him a full transfusion of blood from an immunized dog, hoping that would cover everything. Thankfully it did, because after caring for these puppies for weeks, we were very attached. We decided to keep all three. Jack went to live with my sister in Seattle, and Jenny and Jeffrey stayed in Carmel

with me.

We scattered Jonathon's and Jiminy's ashes around the ice plant atop a sandy knoll along the path we take to the beach every day—year after year. It has grand views that stretch from Pebble Beach to Point Lobos, and is a wonderful place to watch setting suns and rising moons, changing tides and shifting sands, and rainbows and fogbows.

From here one can see the waters churn as migrating whales, long-beaked dolphins, seals, sea otters, and prehistoric pelicans lunge-feed on anchovies and mackerel amidst absolute bird chaos. And from here, one can see unfolding beach scenes and coastal sights; the morning bagpiper who practices in the pre-dawn hours so he won't bother anyone; the board surfers, boot campers and ball players; golfers and dog walkers; picnickers and partiers, and kite flyers and kelp.

Jeffrey, Jack, and Jenny – Photo by: Miranda Wheeler

Jenny and Jeff playing with kelp on Carmel Beach – Photo by: Alexandra Verville

Carmel Beach

Why don't they clean up the kelp? People ask this question a lot, and I have several ready answers. The scientific answer is that kelp forests are the rainforests of the sea, providing food for sea urchins and abalone, and habitats for sea otters and hundreds of species of fish. So kelp washing up on the beach is the sign of our healthy ecosystem. And healthy beaches are meant to have drying and decomposing plants which return nutrients to the natural environs. The practical answer is that, we don't have to clean it up because eventually the ocean washes it away. And, the less obvious answer is that kelp is a wonderfully versatile toy!

Children turn giant bull kelp into jump ropes, snapping bullwhips or doll heads. Or, they race down the beach jumping on the gas bladders that keep kelp afloat—popping them like bubble wrap. And they decorate their sandcastles and mermaids with it. Jenny and Jeff pick up the long thick strands of kelp, and use them as pull-toys. They pull and tug on the kelp rope, and eventually end up side-by-side—galloping down the beach like a pair of perfectly matched bit-trained ponies.

Piles of kelp are also mighty fortresses that one can hide behind, and pounce from, or beat a retreat to for safety. Jenny adores Jeffrey and spends endless beach time trying to get his attention. Jeffrey is usually engaged in the serious business of chasing birds or bugs and their shadows. Jenny hides behind piles of kelp watching him approach, and pounces when he gets close. He ignores her. She then picks up a strand of kelp—one with big brown leaves that wave in the breeze and races past him, clipping him on the shoulder trying to instigate a game of chase. He ignores her. So she brings the kelp to me, trying to make him jealous. We both ignore her. Finally, after she's tried every beguiling trick in her book, she gives up and goes off to play with some other dog. Invariably,

Jeffrey gets jealous and brings her a piece of kelp and off they go, racing down the beach together, side-by-side. When Jeffrey wants to get Jenny's attention, he rolls in the carcass of a dead thing washed ashore and shrouded in kelp, and for some reason, Jenny finds freshly scented Jeffrey irresistible! Honestly, if I had Jenny and Jeff when I was a teenager, I would know everything I needed to know about girl-boy interactions.

Another question people ask a lot goes something like this: "Last year I was here and walked to a secret cove past those rocks. Did Pebble Beach build a wall to keep us out?"

My first instinct is to say, "No, don't be ridiculous," and carry on with kelp games. Instead, I launch into my own explanation of moons and tides and shifting sands. In winter, when the moon is full and close to the earth, the high tides are higher and the low tides are lower; the winds are gustier, the ocean wilder and the current stronger, so the crashing waves pull the sand out to sea, exposing rocky outcroppings that were covered in summer, but exposed in winter and now jut out and block access to the cove.

Then for good measure, I start talking about how JJ love to chase birds who lead them to the edge of these algae-covered rocky outcropping, where I'm irrationally afraid they will slip and fall into a cavern just as a sneaker wave crashes in and shatters them against the rocks.

I'm also irrationally afraid of extendable leashes that I'm sure will somehow get wrapped around JJ's legs, snapping them in two; and of the fishing lures that look like anchovies, which I'm sure JJ will catch in their mouths on the fisherman's back cast and swallow. After sharing these "how will the puppies die today" fears, I get no more silly questions.

Oceanography – Photo by: Kevin D'Angelo

Towns/Criteria	Arcata	Calistoga	Carmel	Capitola	Mendecino	Mill Valley	Murphys	Ojai	Sonoma	Truckee
Family & Friends	No	Yes	Yes	Yes	No	Yes	No	No	Yes	Yes
Scenic Beauty										
Ocean views	Yes	No	Yes	Yes	Yes	No	No	No	No	No
Mountains	No	No	No	Yes	Yes	Yes	Yes	Yes	No	No
Rivers/Lakes		No	Yes	Yes	Yes	No	Yes	Yes	Yes	Yes
Vineyards		Yes	Yes	Yes	Yes	No	No	Yes	Yes	No
Outdoor Activities										
Ocean Sports	Yes	No	Yes	Yes	Yes	No	No	No	No	No
Skiing, Snow	No	No	No	No	No	No	Yes	No	No	Yes
Resort	N/A	Yes	Yes	Yes	Yes	Yes	Yes	Yes	Yes	Yes
Bike, Hike, Camp	Yes	Yes	Yes	Yes	Yes	Yes	Yes	Yes	Yes	Yes
Village Center	11	4	1	3	5	2	9	3	4	10
Walkability	47	83	91	63	61	91	58	86	91	59
Ind Book Store	Yes	Yes	Yes	Yes	Yes	Yes	Yes	Yes	Yes	Yes
NPR Station	Yes	Yes	Yes	Yes	Yes	Yes	Yes	Yes	Yes	Yes
Festivals	Yes	Yes	Yes	Yes	Yes	Yes	Yes	Yes	Yes	Yes
Historic Mission	No	No	Yes	No	No	No	No	Yes	Yes	No
Founding Father	Ben Kelsey, Trail Builder	Sam Brannon, Newspaper	Junipero Sera, Saint	Frederick Hihn, Builder	Henry Meiggs, RR, Lumber	John Reed, Land Grantee	Murphy, Land Grantee	Junipero Sera, Saint	José Altimira, Priest	Chief Truskee, Native
Population	17,231	5,155	3,722	9,919	825	14,350	2,213	7,626	10,648	426
Density psm	1,812	1,997	3,445	5,919	242	3,013	214	1,754	3,883	300
Key Feature	Logging	Hot Springs	All of it	Beach	Ocean Wine	Mt. Tam	Sierra	Shangri-La	Wine	Skiing
Political Rep	D	D	D	D	R/D	D	R	D	D	R

Carmel Village

Some years ago, I created a list of the attributes my *perfect polis* should possess, and a spreadsheet of towns that might have them. Carmel always came out on top having all these in abundance and more—natural scenic village center, walkable streets, aesthetically interesting architecture, an independent bookstore, an NPR station, music, arts and ideas festivals, food and wine festivals, lodging and golf courses for our 4.5 million annual visitors, a historic California mission and a saint for a founding father.

This one square mile town has all of that plus 90 art galleries, 60 coffeehouses, bistros and restaurants, 45 inns, 17,200 gift shops (according to local cartoonist, the late Bill Bates), two grocery stores, one drug store, and a newspaper, the Carmel Pine Cone, widely known for its Police Log.

Carmel residents often call the police for a variety of charming reasons, and these are reported in the Police Log: *squirrel loose in the house; intoxicated man lost his car; elderly lady called the police to plug in her TV because she knew if she did it, she wouldn't be able to get up, and was embarrassed to call the fire department, again*; and our wonderful police respond with good humor.

JJ made the Police Log only once, for a minor singing infraction. In fairness, this ongoing offense usually starts with a police siren, which is like a pitch pipe to JJ—the signal to start singing. Jeffrey hears it and lets out a yap, and then Jenny yips in response, and this yipping and yapping back and forth gradually increases in force and intensity and eventually crests to a harmonic howl. Some neighbors don't think this is funny, and call the police—hence the rap sheet. Other neighbors, the opera singers, local bard and musicians, do think its funny and often stop in front of our gate to sing with the choir.

6:30 AM

At five years old, Jenny and Jeff were fully grown and had well-established habits. Jenny would get up at 6:30 am, lick my face and wiggle along the side of the bed claiming it and everything in it as hers. Jeffrey would swipe a slipper and make for the living room. It was time for our morning romp on the beach.

We'd walk to the ocean at dawn, and watch the colors change from oranges and reds and pinks, to blues and greys and darker greys depending on the time of year, the light and the weather. The sunrises reminded me of a book titled *6:30*, which features a series of Robert Weingarten's photographs. Weingarten set up a camera to take pictures of the beach and ocean horizon, and atmosphere from the same position every morning at 6:30 am. It's fascinating to flip through 362 of these photos and see the range of changing colors.

The sunrises also reminded me of an east coast friend, an artist, who achieved a similar result by swirling watercolors on a page and seeing what came out. He once explained his evolving theory of color and light. Early on, he thought color was serendipitous, so he drew the rough lines but let the color run outside of them. In his next phase, he drew very precisely, and colored inside the lines. Then he moved into his sunrise period—got rid of lines all together and just swirled colors across the paper like an atmospheric wash. What he saw in the atmosphere was what he painted into. So if it was white wash

with a swash of grey across the bottom, he'd add a tiny tree and it became a snowstorm. This technique largely achieved the same effect as the *6:30* photos.

These conversations with old friends in far away places often crossed my mind as JJ raced up and down the beach, chasing birds and bugs, playing with kelp, and begging for cookies. And it occurred to me that Jenny and Jeff were old enough and well-behaved enough that perhaps it was time— time to go visiting.

Texas Riviera

There is never a good time to leave Carmel—except possibly in summer. The fog rolls in and the long days are grey, damp and gloomy. The Texans roll in with the fog, and on June 1, Carmel is transformed into the Texas Riviera. Many Carmelites leave in search of long sunshiny days and warm summer nights. Others leave because they simply don't have anything to wear during *Riviera Season*.

By day, the locals who wear sandy old blue jeans and fleeces make way for Texans speed walking down the beach in their matching florescent pink and blue jogging outfits. At dusk, couples stroll the beach with cocktails in hand—the ladies in long flowing skirts, fisherman knit sweaters and jewels, and the men in leather golf jackets and cowboy boots.

One peek at my wardrobe convinces me that summer is the best time for JJ and me to head out.

Fogbow Carmel Beach – Photo by: Judy Kreger, Monterey Bay Lab Rescue

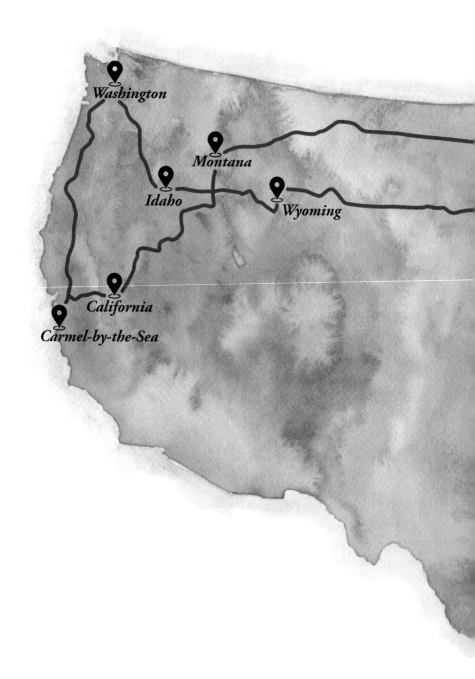

Route Map

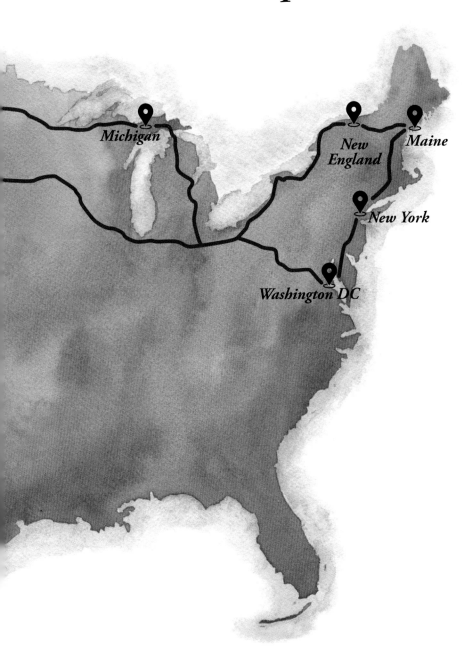

Michigan

New England

Maine

New York

Washington DC

"The man who goes alone can start today; but he who travels with another must wait till that other is ready."
Henry David Thoreau

Road Trips

There are probably as many poems and books written about road trips as there are about our village of Carmel, or fishing or dogs. I've done several road trips, not because I had some need to be free and wander aimlessly and find myself, or because I had some romantic notion that I'd break bread with strangers and find the "real America." I simply wanted to visit friends and family in far away places, and along the way, perhaps I would discover a new way of looking at things.

One of the best things about traveling with JJ was that it was as easy as going alone, and a lot more companionable. Jenny and Jeff watched with anticipation as I packed up our trusty silver Honda CRV with fishing, riding and camping gear, party clothes and house gifts for friends we planned to visit.

JJ weren't sure if they were going on this trip, so they assumed their defensive positions. Jenny slunk onto the couch, crossed her paws and hung her head pathetically over the side. Jeffrey, who has excellent posture, sat ramrod straight staring at me with a toy dangling from his mouth, raising and lowering alternate eyebrows as I continued packing the car. I finally loaded the dog food and dog beds, and their relief was palpable. Once they knew they were coming, Jenny slid off the couch, hoping I hadn't noticed she had been up there, and Jeffrey slouched into a more relaxed lying position—albeit with the toy still clenched and eyebrows still twitching.

With the car packed to the gills, JJ jumped in—ready to go when I was.

Driving Versus Flying

Why do I drive, and not just fly? Airlines take dogs after all. Well, I know that, and I did fly with my first dog. George at one point, but it was simply too stressful.

First I'd have to get him psychologically ready for the trip, since he'd be in a crate for at least six hours. Three months before a trip, I'd pull out the crate, line it with warm comfy blankets and toss in cookies to lure George all the way in. After about three months, he'd invariably have gained several pounds, but was no longer stressed about going into the crate.

The day of departure, we'd go to the airport and I'd take the crate to the dog check-in area and toss in the cookies. George would dutifully crawl in after the cookies and I would close the crate door. He would look at me with those huge soulful brown eyes—as if to say, "I know you are betraying me but I love you anyway."

I'd follow the crate to the cargo area until the handler would let me go no further. I'd then turn and sprint to the departure gate, where I stood glued to the window with my nose on the glass and tears trickling down my cheeks. There was no way I was boarding until I knew the crate was on the plane.

So I'd watch them load the luggage and hear the agent calling my name, telling me I had to board. I'd explain that I couldn't board until I knew for sure the crate was on the plane and I hadn't seen it go on, and could someone please look into the dog section and make sure my golden retriever with the white face was on board. Invariably they would send someone to check, and confirm all was well, and escort me on board, tears and all.

Then we'd take off. Once in the air, I worried about how frightened my dog must be of the noise, and the turbulence—every bump brought more silent tears. A few times, the pilot would come back to see if I was ok. He'd assure me that he'd been down in the hold and all the dogs were warm and resting happily—when really, he should have been flying the plane. The airline people really were quite wonderful.

Finally we'd land. I'd elbow my way through the crowds in a most unladylike manner, and race to the oversized bagged pickup area. In pet flight, it's last on last off, so every oversized item came out first—golf clubs, car seats, skis, musical instruments, sound equipment, entire stages. Finally they would open a door and shove my crate through. I'd open the latch to behold my white-faced golden, alive and well. We'd hightail it out to a patch of grass and heave a sigh of relief.

So there was the trauma of flying dogs, and then there was also the hassle. Once we landed, I'd still have to gather up my luggage, the dog crate, and the dog and head for the car rental shuttle. Invariably, someone on board the shuttle would question whether planes really do have a heated, pressurized dog section, or do they really just load them in with the rest of the luggage. I ignored all of this until one man told a story about the time the heat went off below and the dogs arrived frozen. That was the last time I flew with dogs. Now when I travel with JJ, we drive.

Nevada Billboard – Photo by: Bill Spindler, Southpole Station

Leaving California

The first time we drove across the country, we headed east through Nevada, with visions of Carmel beaches, Sonoma hills and Tahoe lakes still twinkling in our memories. We passed Reno and Mustang Ranch and suddenly we were in the middle of the Nevada desert—wondering why we left.

But this was great country for listening to the *Great Ideas of Philosophy*, 50 lectures by Dr. Daniel Robinson, professor of philosophy and psychology at Georgetown and Oxford. The Nevada lecture was about artificial intelligence, which in short, suggested to me that if one could break an entire legal case down into single bits of informing data, and code the computer to compare those bits to bits of actual law, the artificially intelligent computer could make legal decisions in nanoseconds and we wouldn't need human lawyers at all.

The Nevada Outback

Somewhere near Battle Mountain, Nevada, I switched off the tape and started reading billboards. Apparently, the Washington Post dubbed Battle Mountain "the Armpit of America" and billboard #1 advertised this snooty snub. But ever conscious of its image, Battle Mountain battled back, and the next billboard repositioned the town as… "basecamp to Nevada's outback." Frankly, I was pretty darn impressed. I'd never heard of the Nevada outback, but in an instant, this flat, dusty, tumbleweed-covered desert drive turned into a romantic adventure. So I turned off the highway and headed into the Ruby Mountains.

The Rubies, named for the garnets once found there in abundance by early explorers, are also known as Nevada's Swiss Alps—land of legendary heli-skiing in winter and glorious alpine lake hiking in summer. And for some reason it is a home to the Himalayan Snowcock.

For serious bird lovers like JJ, nothing could be more

serious than a Himalayan Snowcock as they are nearly impossible to catch. At night, they roost at high altitudes and the morning, they wake up and hurl themselves off cliffs, clamping their wings to their sides as they plummet down the mountainside in a free fall to the grasslands below… to feed on insects, plants and seeds.

I considered climbing to higher altitudes to see if we could find a Snowcock, but realized that JJ's only hunting experience was with shorebirds on Carmel beach. They're very good at double-teaming flocks of sandpipers—Jeffrey flushes them off the sand toward Jenny, and Jenny herds them back toward Jeffrey, who chases them until they turn and swoop back toward Jenny. So they never catch anything—it's the joy of the chase. This was the extent of their hunting prowess. I had no confidence that if JJ did see a Snowcock, they wouldn't hurl themselves over the cliff after it. So we stayed low and headed to Ruby Lake to cool off and chase less perilous birds.

As surprising as these mountains were, rising to 11,000 feet straight up from the desert floor, the surrounding ranchlands were equally impressive. Driving along the two-lane road at the base of the mountains, we saw endless views of lush green and gold pasturelands dotted with cattle. There were no visible telephone poles or electric wires or mechanical irrigation systems, and I began to wonder if these ranchers were Amish—or just old ranching families that had been there since the Homestead Act.

Importantly, night was falling and the orange gas-light was on. And since the other thing I didn't see was a gas station, it was time to head to Wells, and trek the rest of this outback on some other safari.

Away from the Rubies, the Nevada desert was hot, hot, hot and dry, and littered with many a blown-out tire. As luck would have it, there was a tire shop next to the gas station in Wells, NV that did a brisk business selling to ignorant travelers simply by pointing out which tires on their parked cars were about to blow.

"Where're ya headed?" asked the giant tattooed man leaning against my front car door.

"Maine." I chirped.

And that's how I got four new tires—as did the nice older couple from Virginia with the small white fluffy dog. We were the sucker cohort.

Ruby Mountain Ranch

Mount Shasta viewed from I-5 – Photo by: Little Mountain 5 CC BY SA 3.0

Oregon, The Siskiyou Trail

On these recent travels with JJ, we traveled north to Portland and Seattle and drove across the top of the country, into the sunrise. This was partly because taking the high road gave us longer cooler days in summer, and partly because there were weddings to attend along the way.

Weddings were only one of the many good reasons to visit Portland and travel the northern route. Another good reason was the drive. It all started with more travels with JJ along the Siskiyou Trail—an old Chinook footpath, later traveled by Hudson Bay trappers, forty-niner gold rushers, and the Central Pacific Railroaders. The trail's romantic history was made more so by its name. Siskiyou might be Chinook for "bob-tailed horse," OR French for six stones as in "six cailloux," OR American for "The Road of a Thousand Wonders." To people in cars with dogs, this old footpath is now known as I-5, and it was far more wondrous than its boring name would suggest.

On a clear day, every turn brought another view of Mount Shasta with its distinctive white-capped peak, and the sight of Mount Lassen looming in the distance.

Suddenly, far off Mount Lassen was joined by Mount Hood and Mount St. Helens. And that's when I realized that all this time we'd been driving into the heart of "The Ring of Fire"—a fiery array of volcanoes that rim the Pacific Ocean—a land of frequent earthquakes.

There's nothing one can do about this concentrated band of earth hazard except possibly… secede from the Union and start a new "State of Jefferson." And in 1941, there was a nearly successful attempt to do just that, by uniting the mountain regions of northern California and southern Oregon into a new 49th state. Rebels barricaded the highways, elected a governor and declared independence. Fortunately the revolution didn't work out, so we were still in the State of Oregon enjoying a sales tax holiday and good old fashion gas station service.

The road dipped down to the small town of Ashland, and our focus shifted from volcanoes to valley life—fishing, rafting, wine and... Shakespeare.

So how did Ashland become a cultural center and home to Oregon's Shakespeare Festival? Well interestingly, back in the late 19th and early 20th century, there was very popular adult education movement in the United States known as the Chautauqua Assemblies. The Chautauqua spread throughout America bringing speakers like William Jennings Bryan, composers like John Philip Sousa, and teachers, entertainers, preacher and others together to educate, entertain and bring culture to rural communities. Ashland residents built a facility to host these events. The movement died out and the building fell into disrepair, but what remained looked like an Elizabethan theater. In the 1930's, a local drama professor proposed using it to present plays by Shakespeare, and the Oregon Shakespeare Festival has been performing them, and other Chautauqua-like events on that stage ever since.

We lingered in Ashland, circled Crater Lake, headed to

Elizabethan Theater – Photo by: Amy Richard

Bend and up to Mount Hood's historic Timberline Lodge. Imagine my surprise to see the parking lot full of cars, chairlifts running, and the mountain teeming with young racers and diehard summer skiers. I thought we had gear packed gear for every occasion, but I was woefully unprepared for summer skiing. So we drove down the mountain and on to Portland—City of Roses.

It's a good thing there were roses, because it was wedding season in Portland—and weddings need roses. Apparently Portland weddings also need goats. Yes, this particular venue, a country club, has a river running through it that waters the blackberry brambles creeping on to the fairways. So a scrappy herd of rented goats lived down by the river protecting the greens by eating the berries. The goats in turn, were safeguarded by rented llamas that spit at the packs of wily coyotes lurking nearby. JJ would have enjoyed this part of the wedding but they weren't invited. Ah Portlandia.

Wedding Roses – Courtesy of: Longfield/Read

Moss Covered Phone Booth, Hoh Rainforest

Washington, Rainforests and Rain Shadows

From the City of Roses to Washington's wetter half, for a few days on the Olympic Peninsula. Why is it wetter? Well, the Olympic Mountains rise up from the sea and block water from storms that blow in from the Pacific—causing about 12 feet of rain every year! All this moisture creates lush, temperate rainforests.

What's the difference between a temperate rainforest and a tropical one—other than temperature—you might ask? Well, tropical rain forests are full of giant trees, tropical birds with bright colorful plumage, giant bugs, chattering monkeys, reptiles and large cats. Temperate rainforests are full of ferns, moss, and giant trees—bigleaf maples, red cedar, giant Sitka spruce, and ancient Douglas fir—primeval sanctuaries for Roosevelt's elk, bears and a host of unseen wildlife

So I packed away the party dresses, pulled out the poncho and headed for the shores of Lake Crescent to meet my sister and JJ's brother, Jack. The Lake is known for its crystal clear waters and abounds with very naïve wildlife. Deer, ducks and rabbits wandered the lawns with impunity and ambled up to JJ and Jack to touch noses, but then thought better of it—avoiding the much-anticipated kerfuffle. Phew! We donned our bathing suits, and fleeces, and ventured off to explore the lakes, waterfalls, rivers, mountains, beaches, glacier capped peaks, and the Hoh rainforest.

According to myth, the Hoh people who lived along the river that runs through the rainforest, were an upside down people who walked on their hands and fished with their feet. When K'wati, the shape-shifting *changer* who went around the world making things as they are today got to the Hoh, he found them hungry and skinny. So he set them right side up and showed them how to operate their nets with their hands. I'm really not sure what happened next but, from the looks of things, he went into the forest and covered everything with moss.

Everything, and I mean everything was covered with moss—tree branches, pathways, picnic tables, phone booths and rolling stones were all covered by 900 different kinds of moss. It was quiet in the forest because all the animals—birds of prey, bears and dinosaurs—had been covered with moss. All the tree stumps were covered with moss, ferns and lichen; and epiphytes (plants that grow on other plants) sprouted all over them.

These stumps are nurseries for new trees, giving them the water, moss thickness, leaf litter, disease protection, nutrients, and sunlight they need to turn into 1000-year-old, 200 foot tall trees. As you might imagine, we were chilled to the bones, and headed out of the rainforest and into what must be a rain shadow—Seattle.

Talk about your sucker days—those abnormally beautiful days that seduce gullible people into believing its always like this. What could be better than spending bright sunshiny days beside sparkling blue lakes, feasting on crabs, giant blueberries and designer coffees; walking with JJ in a specially designed "pet garden" where they paddled through the lily pads and

Concert at St. Michelle Winery, Seattle –
Courtesy of: Dave Littrell, Lakeside Group

rubbed shoulders with swamp dog millionaires. Bright days turned to warm balmy evenings spent with a gathering of young friends under a full moon for an outdoor concert and the music of the night. Sucker day indeed—I'm moving to the Pacific Northwest!

We headed east for a farewell breakfast of blueberry pancakes at a farm 20 minutes from the city, walked through the fields, swam in the river, and got back on the dusty road again. Maybe it really was the "Last Summer on Earth" because the preacher on the radio kept talking about how to raise children for the "Last Days!" Where was my NPR?

Hops Crops

Hops, hops, hops. Hops crops are big in Washington. In fact, 77% of the hop crop in the US is grown right there in the Yakima Valley. If you are among the few of us who still don't brew their own beer, you may not be aware that hops are "bines", obscure perennial vine-like plants that that climb and twist around alpha wires strung like tent cities all over the valley—potential housing for all those suckers who moved to the Pacific Northwest on that sunny day I told you about.

So what do they do with all these hops? Surely hops can be used for something other than beer. Yes indeed they can. Hops are used in herbal medicine as a relaxant and sleep aid. Hops are added to remedies and herbal teas designed to promote healthy sleep—and apparently in many cultures, pillows stuffed with hops are given to people who have difficulty sleeping. Guess what everyone got for Christmas. It may not surprise you to learn that hops and cannabis are both part of the family Cannabaceae. So much for hop heritage.

On through the vineyards and into Washington's wheat fields—which brings me to the subject of… crop circles. Six crop circles appeared in Wilbur, WA in late July, 2012. Some thought there could be an Olympic hoax connection, but six circles are not the Olympic five. And this very dry crop was not crushed, as it would if it had been mechanically flattened. End-of-Days? OR… maybe there is another explanation.

In Tasmania, Australian wallabies were found creating crop circles in fields of opium poppies by running around in circles after consuming some of the opiate-laden plants. So I'm pretty sure hops had something to do with the Washington circles.

I can always tell when JJ are tired of driving. Jenny scooches up from the back seat and gets her front paws on my armrest, and her head and chest between the seats, inching her way slowly forward. Jeffrey gets jealous and also tries to squeeze into the front seat. But, alas, there's no room, so he lies on top of Jenny. So there we were, zipping along with coffee between my knees and two dogs stacked between the seats.

If you're wondering what one does for 12 hours a day in a car traveling mostly across hot dusty plains, I can tell you that this one listens to audiotapes. It isn't long before you understand why the rewind button is considered the greatest boon to learning since the printing press.

Mornings began with my new best friend, Dr. Daniel Robinson, professor of psychology and philosophy at Georgetown and Oxford, whom you first met in Nevada. I was listening to his *Great Ideas of Psychology*. So there we were driving along at an undisclosed clip, JJ stacked and nearly on my lap and Professor Robinson was discussing Franz Joseph Gall, the father of phrenology. Phrenology is a psychological theory based on the idea that parts of the brain are tied to different behaviors, and the larger a specific brain area, the more prominent the associated behavior. Since a baby's skull is soft during gestation, the brain grows and shapes the skull accordingly, so one can actually figure out how people will behave based on the enlarged bumps on their skulls. Apparently Gall would go to cocktail parties and feel guests' skulls—an art/science or parlor game known as bumpology.

Of course this lecture fascinated me. While I listened, I started to wonder whether the expression "that person has a lot of gall" stems from Gall playing bumpology at cocktail parties. I started feeling my own skull to see if there were noticeable bumps indicating abnormal behaviors. Then I felt JJ's skulls, since I figured the kelp bump would be quite apparent. Instead I found a tick and pulled it off and tossed it out the window.

I immediately started worrying about whether a western tick, probably from Big Sur, could become an invasive species and have some detrimental effect on the Washington hops crop, or the Idaho potato crop. Those crops were probably already genetically altered, so then I wondered if they would create some giant mutant tick. And by the time I realized I was drifting, Professor Robinson was three lectures ahead of me. So I simply rewound—and imagined how well I would have done in school if only there had been a rewind button.

Wilber Crop Circles – Photo by: Kevin and Leann Leyva

Stanley Sawtooth Mountains – Photo by: Michael Gordon CC BY SA 3.0

Idaho, Famous Potatoes

We drove on to Idaho and up into the Boise National Forest to beat the heat. This scenic byway wound through miles and miles of lodgepole pines and past old mining towns nestled therein.

It was hot hot hot, but thunderstorms were brewing and I could see white clouds accumulating beyond the mountains. It wasn't cooling down, but there was hope. And then I saw the all too familiar orange gas warning light go on. We were 59 miles from the nearest civilization. OOOPS! I leaned forward in my seat, gripped the steering wheel and kept my foot lightly on the gas to maintain a steady pace, believing that somehow this concentrated tension would conserve gas and get us to the top of the hill, and then gravity would take us the rest of the way. And it worked.

We crossed over the pass and coasted down into the valley—into the Stanley Basin, where I could refill the gas tank and JJ could romp in grassy fields and cool off in spring creeks, and we could see what was really going on. Apparently

the looming thunderstorm created a dry lightning strike, causing yet another major Idaho wildfire.

Wildfires are not all bad. In fact, lodgepole pine forests rely on fire for regeneration. Lodgepole pine stands are so densely populated that they self-thin, leaving dead trees which create fuel for fires. Once the fire reaches the crowns of the trees, it jumps from tree to tree and becomes unstoppable. These fires open the pinecones and release the seeds... creating new growth.

Wildfire outside of Stanley, Idaho

JJ and I fortified ourselves with a stack of Stanley sourdough pancakes, hiked around Redfish Lake and then up to Galena pass for what would have been breathtaking views of the Sawtooth Mountains but for the smoky haze. So we headed south to Ketchum and the Wood River—from the lifecycle of the lodgepole pine, to the lifecycle of the mayfly.

Wood River Valley

I lived in Ketchum for a period while transitioning away from Wall Street and toward the Potomac. Wall Street is a young man's game, and I was neither young nor male, so I thought it was time take a break and think my future through again.

My very loose plan had been to wander through the Rockies, get healthy, find my soul mate, and read the classics—Homer's *Iliad* and *Odyssey*, Ulysses, Faust, *War and Peace*, *One Hundred Years of Solitude*, *Anna Karenina*, all of Shakespeare, *The Lives of a Cell*, and *the Federalist Papers* for starters. My New York colleagues didn't think that sounded like much of a plan, and pushed for details. So I fleshed out the vision for them.

I would go to Ketchum, buy a small business, and live in an executive log cabin on the river, where I would catch fish and pick potatoes and lettuce from my garden for dinner. After dinner, as the vision goes, friends would gather around the campfire and we'd jam.

I thought it was a pretty compelling vision until—and I am not making this up—one co-worker wanted to know who all the people were that would be coming to this after-dinner jam session. I explained that these people would be friends I would have time to make now that I wasn't working all the time. Another asked if these new friends would bring their own instruments to the jam session. I had to explain patiently that these imaginary instruments would be in the imaginary closet in the imaginary log cabin, and that my musical ability also existed only in my imagination. And there was of course the inevitable question, "so how did you decide on Ketchum—one potato two potato?" I was clearly leaving a world dominated by shortsighted men. They simply didn't understand the importance of getting caught up in a vision!

Of course, the reality of life in Ketchum was not at all

like the vision, but it was great just the same. I discovered that most local businesses did not need to be profitable because they were either "toy businesses" started for fun, or concerns funded by profitable entities that needed offsetting losses. I was not one of those entities, so I did not buy a small business.

Executive log cabins turned out to be way too expensive, so I lived in a condo. I made friends and fished, and rafted the rivers. I skied, skated and snow-shoed into the wilds for yurt dinners or Dutch oven cookouts. And I certainly got healthy, read a few classics, and hiked through all those glorious mountains under summer suns and winter snowfalls with my new soul mate, who came in the form of an old golden retriever named George.

Now with JJ, we began the trip down memory lane—

hikes to alpine lakes, visits to Frenchman's Bend hot springs and Silver Creek, and strolls along the banks of the Wood River; stopping now and then to drop a line in the water. My casting is pretty erratic since I worry that Jeffrey, with his bug fetish, might try to catch my fly. So I rarely catch anything. But like Robert Travers (*Testament of a Fisherman*) I too love the environs where trout are found, which are invariably beautiful. And I love being out there with JJ, catching nothing.

Silver Creek Preserve, Bellview, Idaho

Grand Teton Barn – Photo by: Pixabay CCo

Wyoming, Cowboy Country

We left the memories and the fires and wandered through the wilds of Idaho; across the Craters of the Moon, a weird and oddly scenic landscape of volcanic rock, lava flows, scattered islands of cinder cones and sagebrush; through Driggs and Swan Valley, home to Idaho's very rare Trumpeter Swans—and over the Tetons.

The Tetons are very grand indeed and jaw-droppingly beautiful, and we spent some time hiking them. At sunrise, they'd light up from top to bottom, revealing touches of snow and spring green grassy slopes thick with wildflowers. Here spring, summer and fall seemed to peak together in July, so the wildflowers emerged all at once in full bloom. And they were larger than life—honeysuckle flowers the size of magnolias and larkspur the size of gladiolas. Oversized wildflowers attracted oversized bugs—fodder for JJ when they caught them.

The weather was very hot, and strong winds gusted suddenly though those high-mountain passes. It was time to get off the mountain because a thunderstorm loomed, and lightning would strike and either kill you and your dogs, or make you brilliant according to the odd mix of all the "struck by lightning" book and movie memories that suddenly flowed into my mind; *A Match to the Heart* by Wyoming author Gretel Ehrlich, who was struck by lightning while walking her dogs on the mountain; *Phenomenon* where John Travolta gets struck by lightening and becomes brilliant; and of course Mel Gibson's jolt that lets him hear women's inner thoughts—certainly a form of brilliance; and *Powder*, the story of an albino man with an incredible intellect who was struck by lightning in the womb. All this from a mind that never remembers anything.

The Yellowstone–Teton region is extraordinary; a unique creation of ancient volcanoes and glaciers. In fact, Yellowstone is arguably one of the largest active volcanoes in the world—a super volcano! WHAT? It looks nothing like a volcano. It's not a mountain, but rather a vast 1500 square mile depression—a *caldera* formed by a major eruption that led to the collapse of the mouth of the volcano.

Beneath the Yellowstone caldera is a vast chamber of molten rock, and gasses that fuel its spewing geysers, gurgling mud pots and colorful steaming hot springs. The last major eruption of the Yellowstone caldera was over 600,000 years ago, and it ejected 8000 times the ash and lava of Mount St. Helens. The next eruption is 60,000 years overdue—hmmmm.

Yellowstone was designated the world's first national park in 1872, launching a concept that has spawned thousands of national parks in countries around the world. National parks—definitely one of America's greatest ideas. And now, America's national parks have come up with another great idea. If you are over 62, you can get a Golden Ages or senior pass that gets you into every National Park in the country, and most National Forests for the rest of your life—for $10. Think of it—worlds of wonder, spectacular geographic diversity, and wildlife in stunning numbers—for the rest of your life. All for $10. Guess what else everyone got for Christmas.

We stopped in Dubois, WY (pronounced here as "do boys" in the not-so-very-French style), gateway to Wind River country, which in turn is the gateway to Yellowstone country and Teton country to the west, and the Powder River basin country to the east—outlaw country.

Off to Kaycee, WY and Hole in the Wall Ranch—the wild wild west at its civilized best.

Old Faithful Rainbow – Flicka CC BY GNU Free Doc Lic

Great Prismatic Spring – Photo by: Broken Inaglory CC BY SA 3.0Lic

Cowboys riding the red rocks – Courtesy of: Longfield/Wold

Outlaw Country

We headed out of the Wind River Canyon, and onto the windy plains—an arid, high desert of scrub and short grasses, dry washes, wind mills and wild open spaces, where the deer and the antelope play. The vistas were expansive, but only slightly hidden from view was a compelling landscape of red rock formations—layers of sands and sediment that have been cemented into sandstone by iron oxide with some calcium carbonate.

I know this because I listened to my host's increasingly not-brief-but-still-fascinating overview of the geology and history of the Powder River Basin, while standing in the middle of teepee rings that overlook the buffalo jump and grassy green fields that the river flows through. I'd hear it all and almost immediately I'd begin to forget, which was a terrible shame because the truth is… that was about all the geology I knew, and I *wanted* to remember. For some reason, when you see this architectonically designed landscape, it makes you want to head straight to the *Teaching Company* to order *Nature of Earth* and take the course on geology.

Surrounded by red rocks, and green grassy meadows, the dogs rolled around to cover themselves with the local scent. They do this everywhere, presumably so other dogs won't know they're tourists.

Smothered in the spirit of the place, they stared in wonder as I threw a line into the crystal clear spring creeks, and we all watched wily old fish mock my fly as they munched on tiny shrimp and watercress. Jeffrey loves to fish and

Steamboar Rock – Courtesy of: Wold/Longfield

fishes like a bear… staring into the stream and either swiping at passing fish with his paw, or pouncing on them in the water. Jenny crouches down beside the stream waiting for Jeffrey to toss her a fish. Needless to say, we could trash a hole pretty quickly, so we never fished until others had passed through.

After fishing, we would pack a picnic lunch and hike up to the top of Castle Rock or Steamboat, or perhaps down to Outlaw Cave. We were in the heart of outlaw country after all, home of the Hole-In-The-Wall-Gang and site of the Johnson County Wars.

A few years ago, my hosts discovered the ruins of a log cabin down by the river, which turned out to be Nate Champion's hideout. Wyoming history is replete with English cattle barons running their large herds over what had been free range until the homesteaders arrived. Once the homesteaders arrived and put their cattle on the same land, there were mix-ups. The cattle barons, who ran thousands of cattle, had a habit of claiming all unbranded calves as their own, exacerbating the tension between the large and small operators.

Nate Champion, a homesteader and righteous cattle rustler, stood up to the cattle barons and became a key figure in the Johnson County Wars. This cabin was the site of one of the many shootouts between Nate and the Wyoming Stock Growers Association's boys, and another landmark for the range wars that have since become symbolic of the Wild West and the expansion into the American frontier.

We continued our rendezvous with history, hiking over to the next ranch to see the actual hole-in the-wall, which is not hole at all, but rather a V in the wall—a narrow pass in the red rock wall formation that stretches for miles. Outlaw gangs would herd their stolen cattle and stash their gold on the other side of the wall and hide out. From a perch by the V, they could easily spot approaching lawmen, so the hideout was easy to defend.

The rest of our visit was wonderful, so much to do and learn—like how to herd grasshoppers into Sheep's Creek so fish would jump and we'd know where to cast, and where to search for petrified squid and buffalo bones and arrow heads. We'd saddle our horses and round-up stray calves; play a couple rounds of cowboy golf before dinner; mosey on up to Poker Creek for canoeing and cocktails; cook up bounty from the garden for 15-20 people every day; and after dinner we'd sing around the player piano, play some paddle tennis and hike to the top of the hill to see the "Lights of Barnum," which turned out to be lights from three trailers, the only civilization for miles around.

Or, we'd sit around the fire gazing at full moons and falling stars while listening to Buck Cunningham stories like, "horses are in the high meadows and haven't been rode much, so they're a bit *bucky*—could 'a been spooked by a cougar. So Buck set a trap and caught one by the toe! It was ragin' mad so he took a bear trap and clapped it round its neck and kilt it, But where there's one there's more."

I figured they made up these stories to astound me, but there *was* a new addition this time—Charlotte the stuffed cougar was crouching on the high cross beam in the great room, ready to pounce on the dining room table. I didn't check her toes.

JJ loved ranch life, but the more time we spent there, the more I realized they really were tenderfoot "Texas Riviera" dogs. I envisioned days of riding through the fields together with Jenny and Jeff frolicking dutifully behind my horse. But if they saw me mount a horse, they started to worry and whimper and tried to climb up with me—not a good idea with those *bucky* mustangs.

So instead, JJ chased deer and antelope through the fields and up the rocky cacti-covered hills, and came back with thistles in their fur and thorns in their paws. They wanted to run with the ranch dogs and help herd the cattle from one field to the next, nipping at their heels and leaping over and under their flying hind legs. But in a flash of the familiar *how will the puppies die today* moment, I said no, and I think they were relieved just to watch.

We took one last romp through the meadows before we left, and Jenny and Jeff got... *skunked.* There is a very effective skunk spray removal formula that involves a combination of:

1-quart hydrogen peroxide,
1 tsp. dishwashing detergent and
¼ cup baking soda.

But we were 30 miles from the nearest hydrogen peroxide and had to settle for strawberry scented shampoo. I bathed them and rinsed them in the river, and we ran through the fields trying to dry off. Then I loaded a couple of strawberry-skunk-scented dogs into the back seat and we headed down the road... with the windows open.

Jenny and Jeff skunked

Nebraska Wheat Fields – Photo by: USDA.gov

Across the Great Plains

On the road again—the car still caked in red ranch dust from driving through Wyoming's wild open spaces and red rock formations—and into the Great Plains.

We headed east on I-80 into Nebraska and Iowa, past field after rolling green field of corn—miles and miles of corn, hundreds of miles of corn, wheat, beans and gluten-free sorghum. I imagined these fields were strategically planted in patchwork patterns that sent messages to those with a birds-eye view of the cornfields. The message was that we were deep into the breadbasket of America.

Jenny and Jeff were hot and apparently bored, since once again they were stacked between the seats. I tried explaining to them that stacking would only increase their body heat and discomfort, but they had a point to make and they were making it. So I started looking for a watering hole—a place for them to swim and cool off. And suddenly, I saw them. Watering holes were everywhere… right off the highway.

I discovered that when I-80 was built, the developers chose the easy, cheap route through the flat, wide-open Platte River Valley. There were no hills to provide fill material, so the road builders dug pits and borrowed the fill from the valley floor. Knowing that groundwater would seep into these "borrow pits," engineers and fishery biologists collaborated to make sure the pits were dug as proper fishing holes. There are now more than 50 clear, deep, fishing lakes along I-80 in Nebraska—perfect for anglers, and great swimming holes for hot dogs.

How did the developers know the groundwater would seep into the borrow pits? Well it turns out that Nebraska sits right on top of the Ogallala Aquifer, the largest underground reservoir in the United States. So it's the Ogallala Aquifer that gives life to these fields and millions of acres of grasslands, making the Great Plains… really great!

This is soft, gentle country. It's a place where people with corn-fed values and an entrepreneurial spirit are planting windmills and several NPR station towers thank heavens, right there in the middle of the cornfields. I predict Nebraska and Iowa will quietly emerge as net energy producers in a few years.

Orphan Trains

Windmills in Iowa cornfields

I know this sounds corny but… I love Nebraska and Iowa with their fields of dreams; their red barns and silos and windmills; romantic covered bridges (of Madison County); and of course their adorable Orphan Trains. WHAT? Yes, Orphan Trains.

Did you know that at the turn of the last century Orphan Trains from New York "placed out" 150,000 to 200,000 children (infants to 15 years old) mainly to homes in the farming communities of the Midwest? Some were orphans, many were street kids, runaways and gang members, and others were from destitute families unable to care for them. The idea was to get them off the streets and into farm families who would care for them in exchange for help on the farm. Sometimes it worked—two Orphan Train kids became governors of South Dakota and Alaska. And sometimes it didn't—Billy the Kid was an Orphan Train boy. The things you learn.

I saw a sign for a town called Anita (my mother's name) and turned off the highway. Anita's motto is "A Whale of A Town," which is hard to be when only 266 families actually live there, and there is no ocean, let alone whales. But it does have a State Park with a beautiful lake. So we stopped to cool off and stretch our legs and walk the four-mile path around the lake—a lovely way to spend a soft summer afternoon.

Lickety-split through Illinois, Ohio and over the Appalachians. No longer mesmerized by the Great Ideas of Philosophy, I switched to NPR, and finally found Diane Rheam, who was talking to an author about… of all things… drawing.

The woman was saying that anyone could learn to draw well if they just tap into the right side of the brain, the spatial side. Apparently the way to do this is by… *drawing upside down*. So I pulled over to test this theory and tried to draw a telephone pole, but it did not turn out well at all. I may need to read the book because I couldn't figure out whether drawing upside down meant you should draw from the bottom up, or literally turn the image around in your head, and assuming you could do that, how do you keep it there? And if I could learn to draw this way, perhaps a similar theory could be applied to singing… and how would that work? These are the things I think about while driving through great wide-open spaces with JJ stacked between the seats.

Still unable to draw or sing, we drove, down through Pennsylvania and Maryland and on to Prime Hook and the Delaware shore… all the way from Sea to Shining Sea.

Prime Hook Birds – Photo by: Bart Wilson/USFWS Northeast Region CC BY 2.0

Delaware, Prime Hook

Corn, corn, corn, soybeans, corn, corn, and suddenly—there were peach trees and lavender fields and raspberry patches and beach plums, or "pruim" as they were called by the early Dutch settlers. Apparently, the settlers were so taken with the beach plums, they called this lovely corner of Delaware Prium Hoek, or Plum Corner. Prium Hoek has since corrupted into Prime Hook.

Prime Hook has become a national wildlife refuge—the last stop for east coast migratory birds on their way to the arctic. The refuge's freshwater wetlands and salt marches host migrating shorebirds that feast on the eggs of spawning horseshoe crabs—primitive ancient scorpion-like creatures that have five pairs of legs, medicinally valuable blue blood, and several pairs of eyes on the head, *plus* extra eyespots under the shell and on their spike-like tail.

JJ and I awakened to the music of the marsh—the singing birds, flapping wings, rustling leaves and softly breaking waves—wafting through the open window. We took a long lingering walk down the beach, flipping horseshoe crabs upright so they could claw their way back into the bay, while keeping their extra eyespots on the dogs, who found them most curious.

Horseshoe Crab – Photo by: Pos Robert, USFW

When the moon was full, and the tide at its lowest, we'd swim with the dogs out to the sandbar, a favorite gathering place for this small beachside community in happier times. Unfortunately, rising tides and heavy storms breached the dunes, and salt water flowed freely into this stunning freshwater marsh, creating dead zones and ruining crops of neighboring farmers.

This beach community was small, but like all communities, these people cared about their homes and these wetlands, and set about to actively *encourage* U.S. Fish and Wildlife Service and the Delaware's Department of Natural Resources and Environmental Control to repair the dune breaches and restore the marsh. It took an even greater calamity in the form of Hurricane Sandy to drive home the fact that coastal wetlands, tidal marshes and barrier islands are an important buffer against giant storms and rising sea levels. *Did we not learn anything from Katrina?*

Finally, bringing back these wetlands became a priority, and it was Sandy's disaster relief fund that provided the money to restore Prime Hook National Wildlife Reserve's tidal marsh. Happily, all is now as it was meant to be in Plum Corner.

Prime Hook Marsh Restoration – USFW Service Northeast Region, CC BY 2.0

Longview Views – Courtesy of: McIlvaine/Breese

Maryland, Longview Farm

Off the sandbar and over the Bay Bridge to Accokeek, Maryland for Sunday supper on the porch at Longview Farm—so named because of its long and lovely views up the Potomac River to Washington DC straight ahead, and down river to Mount Vernon off to the left.

On this farm, located 20 minutes from the White House, bald eagles nested in the woods and deer, foxes and wild turkey were in residence.

It's always intriguing to see how people stay engaged as they pull away from lifelong careers and follow new callings. On the west coast, people tend to play golf, or go fishing and become guides. Or, they go on bike rides—long *double century* bike rides down the coast, around the lakes and through the vineyards—Italian vineyards, where Bose speakers play Mozart and Bach to make the grapes happier. Happy grapes in turn lull energetic bike riders into a blur of Bose and Bach and breathtaking food, so they take Italian cooking classes, build a pergola, buy a vineyard and take up viniculture.

On the east coast, people tend to start foundations, write books, become Knights, and blog. Some attend mob-grazing

57 Chevy Truck – Courtesy of: McIlvaine/Breese

conferences, so they can raise cows that feed on organic grass and kelp, and pigs that forage through oak and poplar woods for grubs and acorns. They join the farm-to-table movement and grow organic vegetables and free-range chicken eggs on gentleperson farms, and deliver them in person inside the Beltway in an old '53 Chevy truck for:

> Eggs @ $5 a dozen
> Chutney @$5 a jar
> Heirloom Tomatoes @ $3.75/lb
> Basil @ $1 for 5 sprigs
> Chickens @ $4.25/lb
> Italian hot sausage loose @$6.25/lb

On this porch, family friends and fireflies gathered to feast on summer salads of heirloom tomatoes with burrata, torn croutons, and opal basil straight from the garden—plus the proverbial corn, peaches and plums from Plum Corner!

And out in the field, a group that joins great chefs with local farms around the world was setting up long tables in the lavender field down by the old tobacco shed. No corn and peaches here. This meal was to be an unusual blend of Taiwanese pork sausage with ginger, garlic and chilies, and Cambodian street food seasoned with the hottest of peppers; Carolina reaper, Trinidad scorpion, and ghost peppers.

Outstanding in the Field—connecting diners to the land and the origins of their food, and honoring the local farmers, artisans and exotic chefs who cultivate it—such a great concept.

Outstanding in the Field Dinner – Courtesy of: McIlvaine/Breese

United States Capitol

Washington DC, City of Trees

Off the farm and over the bridge to Washington DC we drove. California may be home, but DC will always be a special place, because of friends there and a thousand memories we made together. Most of these friends had headed north to cooler climes or east to the beaches, fleeing DC's summer heat and humidity. So JJ and I had the place pretty much to ourselves.

Washington DC, has been called many things: "Our Nation's Capital," "The American Rome," "The District," "City of Magnificent Intentions" (Charles Dickens), and "New York's Studious Cousin," to name a few. But the one that struck me has always been… "The City of Trees." The first time I visited, I was struck by the gleaming white, monumental buildings floating atop a vast carpet of trees. It's a gorgeous city.

Every street is lined with trees, and there are so many parks and gardens all seemingly linked to each other, so that from above, the town looks more like forest than a heavily populated city. And the view from beneath the canopy is just as lush. I could walk on paths through the woods from my home in NW Washington all the way to The Mall without crossing a street and barely touching a sidewalk. And along the way, see all manner of wildlife—songbirds, golden eagles, red and silver foxes, deer, turtles—right there in the woods, seven minutes from the White House.

So that's just what JJ and I did. We walked through Battery Kemble Park and down to the C&O Canal, which stretches 184 miles from Georgetown to Ohio. It's an easy walk along the towpath where oxen once trod, pulling barges laden with lumber, coal and agricultural products along the watery road, through 75 locks and past 200 year-old stone gatehouses.

We strolled through Georgetown, past the waterfront,

under the Kennedy Center, around to Memorial Bridge and up the Watergate steps to "The Mall," spelled with a capital T and a capital M, which is how you know it's *so much more* than a shopping mall.

The Mall is another one of our amazing National Parks. It is that vast grassy expanse that connects Capitol Hill to the Lincoln Memorial, and the Whitehouse to Jefferson Memorial. It houses a myriad of monuments, gardens, statues and eleven of the Smithsonian's nineteen museums and galleries. WHAT? I thought the Smithsonian was a museum—a one-building museum—specifically that iconic red sandstone building popularly known as The Castle. But with all those exhibition halls and galleries, nine research centers and the National Zoo, the Smithsonian is so much more. The Castle was the first Smithsonian building, but it isn't all that big so it couldn't possibly hold all of America's treasures. Maybe it did in the beginning, but today it houses the welcome center and administrative offices.

JJ were not welcome in the museums, so we splashed in the fountains, and picnicked on the grass near one of several *skylights* that let natural light flood down into the warren of

Smithsonian Castle

subterranean offices and tunnels that lie beneath The Mall. All the buildings in the United States Capitol Complex and Library of Congress are connected by tunnels and underground walkways providing easy passage for legislators. And, as we all know from political thrillers, the White House has its own tunnels and underground command center bunker. So, too, The Mall. Ah DC, "City of Tunnels."

JJ and I also were not welcome in the tunnels, so we headed back to the river and through the woods to our home away from home in Ward 3, a section of Northwest DC. For those who aren't familiar with DC, it is divided into eight Wards or neighborhoods for electoral and administrative purposes.

Mine was a neighborhood inhabited largely by journalists, lawyers, librarians, diplomats, congressional staffers, spies, artists, historians and policy wonks. As David Brooks explained in his NY Times article *Ward Three Morality*, "These people are all very nice and cerebral. On any given Saturday, half the people in Ward 3 are arranging panel discussions for the other half to participate in." New York's studious cousin indeed. They live in modest homes among the trees, where they do their own gardening and clean their own gutters. It's not that they can't afford help, but for Ward 3 people, hard work is part of their tradition—part of their character. And they do it with ritual grace. The only time I ever saw my 85-year old neighbor, a former diplomat, remove his jacket was when he came over to chop and stack my firewood.

For me, DC will always be, as Wallace Stegner said, "the place where during the best time of our lives, friendship had its home and happiness its headquarters."

Plaza Hotel Reflection

New York, The Big Apple

Out of the "City of Trees" and up the NJ Turnpike toward Manhattan—New York City, "The Big Apple." So why do they call it The Big Apple? Well, according to the Etymology Dictionary, the earliest known usage of The Big Apple appeared in 1909 in a book entitled, *The Wayfarer in New York*. In it, Edward Martin wrote that, "Kansas is apt to see in New York a greedy city... It inclines to think that *the big apple* gets a disproportionate share of the national sap." Jazz musicians agreed and began using "*apple*" to refer to any city, especially a northern one. Either way, the expression was popularized by a Big Apple tourism promotion campaign that was going on when I first arrived.

Yes, in a youthfully enthusiastic career move, I traded my poppy-and-lupine-covered California hills for the *sturm* and *drang* of New York. It was the early 1970's and the City was in one of its cyclical down periods at the time. Its economy had been devastated by the decline of manufacturing and the flight of the white middle class to the suburbs. Central Park, a masterpiece of landscape architecture was in a state of disrepair—dusty by day and dangerous at night—vandalism, illicit activities, and gangs commandeering open space made the Park inaccessible to most. Graffiti covered the subways, the streets were dark and gritty, and rat-infested garbage piled-up on the sidewalks during strikes.

All I saw was opportunity… and warm summer nights. That won't mean much to anyone who wasn't raised in the foggy San Francisco area, but I'd always dreamed of going out to dinner in summer without having to wear a woolen cloak. And in New York, that was possible.

Rents were low and I lucked into a brownstone studio in the 70's off Madison. This was key because at the time, busy people could easily classify you in three questions or less—Where do you work? Where do you live? Where did you grow up? A person could discern that I was in finance, lived on the then-popular Upper East Side, and had questionable judgment—having made the unthinkable move from west to east

If JJ and I were to visit my old haunts, we knew we really should touch base in New York… and touching base on a hot summer day was about all JJ could handle. We headed over the George Washington Bridge and took a quick detour into town and through my lovely tree-lined neighborhoods. Skylines change, but I'm pleased to say, old brownstones never do.

New York has been evolving since the 80's, and much to my amazement had become surprisingly dog friendly. JJ and I could have done much more than we did. We could have walked around Ground Zero, across the Brooklyn Bridge, and through Grand Central Terminal. And, if we had been there during *dog fashion week*, we could have headed to The Shops at Columbus Circle where JJ could have enjoyed foie gras dog biscuits from Bouchon Bakery, and I could have dined alfresco, and cloakless.

Alas, New York was noisy, hot and humid and I didn't think we three would have enjoyed sightseeing or shopping. So we headed to Central Park for an unsatisfying on-lease romp. When JJ saw their first NY dog walker coming toward them with twelve or more large and small charges on leash, they froze. JJ love their own Carmel pack, but these were clearly un-vetted packs, and there were several headed toward us. Seriously outnumbered, it was time to

78th Street Brownstone

skedaddle—escape these gangs of New York and head out to the Connecticut woods, to find the source of the national sap.

New York Dogwalkers – Photo by: Nancy B. Turner

Norfolk Library – Carol M. Highsmith
Archive collection at *the Library of Congress*

Connecticut, Land of Steady Habits

Heading north on I-95, we drove past New York's loveliest bedroom communities and Connecticut's picturesque coastal villages. Years ago, when the cool New Yorkers headed to the Hamptons, I would go to Connecticut—"Land of Steady Habits"— to get grounded.

We turned west toward the Litchfield Hills and the tiny village of Norfolk to stay at the farm with longtime DC friends. Known as the "icebox" of Connecticut, it is the highest point in the state and was a refreshing 7 degrees cooler than anywhere we'd been. Thus revived, it was hard not to notice the stately architecture and cultural tone of the place; a legacy of the town's founding families. We drove past the village green with its white spired and granite churches, and past magnificent historic buildings, dating back to the mid-1800's: the Shingled-style Library; Infinity Hall and the Sports Barn with its "real tennis" court.

For you tennis enthusiasts, real tennis, also known as court tennis or royal tennis in Australia and England, is the original racquet sport from which the modern game of "lawn tennis" evolved. The French call it courte paume, a reference to jeu de paume—the original handball. But wait! Isn't the Jeu de Paume a Parisian arts center—the museum that once housed the important impressionist works? Yes it is. And it was originally constructed in 1861 during Napoleon's reign, to house real tennis courts. In real tennis, the building is the court. Walls on all four sides—with spectator galleries, sloping roofs and buttresses, off of which shots can be played—enclose the court. As far as I can tell, the game is very complex—a mix of squash, tennis, and chess, and as easily explained as cricket!

JJ don't play tennis, real or not, so we continued on to the White House and Music Shed, home of Yale's Summer School of Music and the Chamber Music Festival. This perfect New

Real Tennis Court – Photo by: Nigel Mykura, CC BY SA 2.0

England village lies across the border from the Berkshire Hills in Massachusetts and Tanglewood, the summer home of the Boston Symphony. We were in the heart of summer music festival country.

As we continued up the winding mountain road, I smiled upon seeing the faded blooms of thousands of daffodils that lined it. These friends once confessed to planting daffodil and snowdrop bulbs along the Battery Kemble Park path in DC and along Norfolk's winding roadsides. The story goes, that "this random bulb planting was inspired by a colorful character known as the Hermit of Fontainebleau, who lived in that old and neglected French royal park in the early 19th century. Secretively and surreptitiously he went out every day planting bulbs to reclaim the paths and roads of that park so the public could enjoy them. When the restored Bourbon monarchs tried to reassert their "droit de seigneur" over the park, the outcry from the happy users was so great, that the Royals were forced to relinquish ownership and turn the park over to the people. Long live the people and scurriers of the night!"

JJ and I arrived at the farm and were greeted enthusiastically by our hosts, their chocolate labs and the family cow. After a light lunch of strawberries and zucchini flowers from the garden, we headed immediately to Tobey Pond for a dip. This jewel of a lake is a favored swimming hole and comes with its own 19th-century bathing kiosk, a rustic wooden summerhouse with covered deck overlooking the water, dressing rooms and lounging area—handy for changing clothes, picnics and apparently, naps.

The host labs bolted down the beach and onto the pier, and belly flopped into the water as labs are wont do. JJ are only half-lab and were not wont to do anything of the sort. They tiptoed daintily to the edge of the pier, looked down and retreated. Jeffrey and I trotted over to the sandy shore and waded in from there to swim with the rest of the dogs. Jenny stood close to shore, chest deep in water, brow furrowed and worried about us.

No time for napping, JJ and I headed down the dirt road for a walk through the Great Mountain Forest—a classic example of progressive-era conservationism. In the mid-to-late 1800's, iron companies owned the forest, and overcut it to produce coal for iron smelting, tanbark for tanning, and fields for farming. By the early 1900's the conservationists of Teddy Roosevelt's time realized the country was exploiting its natural resources and ruining the land, and called for an end to the wasteful use of raw materials. In this corner of Connecticut, two local conservationists began buying parcels around the lake and branched out from there. They reintroduced deer, waterfowl and upland game birds and, planted trees. Initially they planned to use this as a hunting camp, which surprisingly … was how many conservation efforts started. Today it's a carefully managed working forest that produces wood, maple syrup and Christmas wreaths; and supports recreation and research on how best to protect watersheds and a healthy wildlife population.

As we wandered through the woods, I was reminded of the long-ago conversation that prompted this journey, about the serendipitous nature of color and light. And in this forest, I saw it. Looked at one way, the forest is nothing but shadows and light splashed over tree leaves, boughs and branches. Looked at another way, it's the stark forms of the trunks and branches that hold and shape the color.

Lost in reverie, JJ and I reached another lake and a cluster of great old buildings that looked like Camp Kilowana, my first overnight scout camp. And that's pretty much what it was—Yale's Forestry Camp, complete with central great rooms for teaching and gathering, and several smaller cabins scattered about for living space. Turns out, those progressive era conservationists I told you about were alumnae who ceded the land and buildings to Yale's pioneering School of Forestry. Yalies must have spent a lot of time summering in Norfolk over the years.

Yale must be a forward thinking institution, because its Psychology Department recently established a Canine Cognition Center. The Center studies how dogs think about the world—how they perceive their environment, solve problems and make decisions. We could have headed to New Haven and volunteered for the program, so Jenny and Jeff could have received Yale diplomas. PhD's from Yale would certainly put to rest any speculation that they weren't brilliant.

Regrettably, we were not summering in Connecticut and didn't have time for PhD's. So we packed up the car, and made our way north.

Great Mountain Forest – Photo by: GMF Forest Manger Jody Bronson

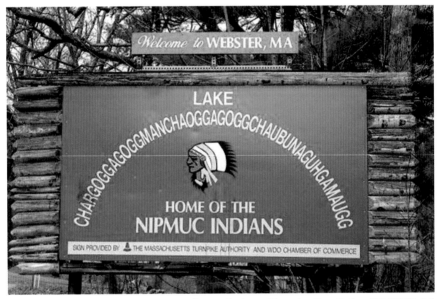

Webster Lake Sign – Photo by: Bree Bailey, CC BY SA 2.0

Massachusetts, Chaubunagungamaug

Over the border to Massachusetts and on to Chaubunagungamaug Lake, pronounced just the way it looks—Char-gogg-a-gogg-man-chaug-gaa-gogg-chau-bun-a-gung-a-maugg—with accents on the second, sixth and twelfth syllables. Yes, it is officially the longest name of anyplace in the US. It's an Algonquian word meaning "you fish on your side, I fish on my side and nobody fish in the middle." Such rich words make me wonder why writers bother making up new languages… like Na'vi for Avatar, or Tolkien Elvish or Klingon, when we already have so many great tongues that largely go unspoken.

The lake is more commonly known as Webster Lake, after Daniel Webster (speaking of words) who was greatly admired by the town founder Samuel Slater.

Slater in turn, was widely known as the "father of the American factory system." The British, however, knew him as "Slater the Traitor." When he arrived in the US in 1789, the US was the world's biggest exporter of cotton, and the country was eager to acquire the spinning technology to process it. The British protected their commercial interests by banning skilled textile workers from emigrating to America. But Slater came anyway—bringing with him the secret to the water-powered spinning machine—and thus bringing the industrial revolution to America.

Not only did Slater bring British textile technology to America, he developed processes that divided factory work into such simple steps, that children aged four to ten could do it… and did. No Orphan Trains for these kids.

So what ever happened to Slater's Mills? Well, Horatio, one of Samuel's sons, took over the business and ran the Webster mill, eventually moving it to South Carolina. And that mill is the very one that made the high-tech materials for the astronaut space suits for the first moon landing, and for the Space Shuttle crews! From Belper, England to the moon... quite a legacy.

We stopped here for a few days at the lake with old friends from London days. A few days at the lake is like time at "cousin's camp." We spent it kayaking with the dogs, who were now duly trained to stay close to shore in the lily pads, rather than following alongside the kayaks and into the deep like sea otters. One of my goals on this trip was to get the dogs into a kayak with me so we could paddle around together, but that would require a bigger kayak and more time.

We would have loved to stay for the summer at Lake Chaubunagungamaug, and might have had to because... I couldn't find Jeffrey. Good grief! He was right behind me. He does this. If we're somewhere he especially likes, he simply hides when its time to leave, and refuses to come. In Big Sur, he hid behind the Loo With a View. In Washington it was the garden shed. In Wyoming, it was the woodpile, and in Norfolk he scrunched down beside the raised garden beds somewhere between the peas and the raspberries. I called and whistled, and he didn't come. So we started checking the obvious places—down by the pier, the kitchen, the cousins' cabin.

Then I noticed Jenny staring at the back of the house, and followed her gaze to the sheets hanging from the clotheslines, absorbing the fresh warm scent of afternoon sun. My host just loves that fresh-from-the-clothesline-smell of clean sheets, and sings a cappella while she pins them up. Apparently, she once tried hanging sheets to dry in their Greenwich garden, but that "steady habit" was quickly quashed by neighbors with different habits.

Jenny and I wandered over to the laundry pile, and there behind the wet sheets I saw Jeffrey's tail twitching. He casually raised his head and seemed genuinely surprised to see me.

"Oel ngti kameie" ('I see you' in Navi) I said, and lassoed him with his leash. We were off to the next place I knew he wouldn't want to leave.

Hanging Laundry – Painting by Jeno Czuk,
Source: Virag Judit Galeria Public Domain

Southport Island, Maine – Photo by: William Sharon Farr Jr.

Maine's Rockbound Coast

Southport Island

Ah bridges—connections to old friends and amazing places—and always the chokepoints. Usually it's traffic flow, construction and accidents that cause the backups. But in Wiscasset, gateway to Boothbay Harbor and Southport, Maine, it's "Red's Eats."

Yes, Red's Eats is located on a crowded corner just before the Wiscasset Bridge. Unable to park, travelers simply jump out of their cars to run in to grab the "best lobster roll" in Maine. And once the first person runs in, everyone else might as well do the same, because no one is moving. Quite a marketing concept—location, location, block traffic.

On to Southport, an island off of Boothbay Harbor that stretches out into Sheepscot Bay.

Maine's jagged rockbound coast was created by glacial activity during the last ice age. When the ice melted, rising sea levels drowned the coast, transforming the hilly land into small islands and inlets, turning valleys into bays and mountaintops into islands. All along the seaboard, fingers of land reach into the ocean creating thousands of miles of coastline—3,478 miles to be exact—whereas, the waterfront distance is less than 300 miles as the crow flies. It is no wonder every home seems to have an ocean view.

We headed over the swing bridge and left over the rickety bridge, down the road along the shore, past charming coastal homes secreted in among the trees until we reached the tip of the island. JJ and I greeted our hosts and then quickly scampered across the boulders to the shore, dipping our toes into the icy blue water, and watching as white sailed-sloops, schooners, ketches and yawls glided in and out of the harbor. The sun started to set, and it was time to gather with friends and neighbors, and feast on lobster and butter, corn and butter, bread and butter, and blueberry muffins… and butter.

The 6:30 am sun streamed through the window and we could hear the seals breathing as the water lapped softly against the rocky coast. The lobstermen were checking their traps, the loons were aoohooooooooing, and JJ were licking my face and smiling broadly. It was time to head into the forest for the morning walk.

The Maine woods are fresh and damp in the early morning and full of wild scents. On these walks, JJ would trot shoulder-to-shoulder, trailing my hosts while I brought up the rear—careful to stay in the protected area between us. They sniffed every leaf and turned every twig—on high alert, lest they encounter the coyote or moose pack that had traveled that path before us. The wild scents must have dissipated during the day, because they behaved differently on the afternoon walks. Jeffrey would race on ahead of the group—chasing anything that cracked a twig, while Jenny ran fore and aft, making sure we were all moving in the same direction. I sometimes wonder if Jenny has some collie in her genes, because she's a bit of a herder, and she worries if anyone straggles.

The Maine woods are also quite enchanting, covered with budding pine trees, red bunchberries, sun-dappled ferns and crystal clear springs trickling through mossy green fields. And just when we thought the forest couldn't get any more magical, we stumbled across a community of *fairy houses.*

In Maine, children build fairy houses and gnome homes in the mossy embankments to attract these small mysterious creatures. They use whatever building materials nature provides—bark and berries, sticks and shells, nuts, pinecones and mushroom caps and moss. Some houses have pebble pathways and names like Oberon, Titania, Aethelwine and Sharon, while others are fairy cabins in the woods… vacation homes I presume. Monhegan Island is particularly famous for its fairy houses and gnome homes, but JJ and I have found (and built) them everywhere from Southport to Mount Desert Island.

So we headed north to look for fairy houses and hopefully find Sauerkraut. On my host's kitchen bulletin board is a tiny clipping from the Boothbay Register. All it says is "Kraut's ready." Ever since 1910 when Virgil Morse first delivered his pickled cabbage to John Gray's store in Waldoboro, locals have loved this fall treat, and have waited eagerly for word that his Kraut was ready. And this tiny ad was the annual announcement. Mainer marketing—unusual and yet effective.

Maine Fairy House

Bass Harbor Lighthouse – Photo by: Albert E. Theberge, NOAA Corps

Mount Desert Island

It's a long lovely drive along the coast from Southport to Mount Desert, but as beautiful as it was, we knew what was in store, and couldn't wait to get to there. So we headed north to Waldoboro to grab some kraut; stopped in Rockland, for a visit to the Farnsworth Art Museum—home to three generations of Wyeth art; through Camden, and then *down east* toward Mount Desert Island.

Mount Desert is the largest island in Maine and home to Acadia National Park and a handful of artful seaside towns that were once, and still are full of "rusticators"—families who came to spend long summers on the rustic coast of Maine.

My version of the history of Mount Desert Island is based on an assumption that all the great summer destinations, east coast and west, were initially places of extraordinary natural beauty, where professors and artists went during their enviably long summer vacations. They traveled by steamer and gathered to exchange ideas, write books and create art, which attracted other artists and interesting people to the community.

In the case of Mount Desert, apparently it was the paintings of Thomas Cole and Frederic Church that caught

JJ romping on Maine lawn

the eye of the barons of the Gilded Age, who wanted to experience this isolated wilderness—and own it—and eventually preserve it. We have these barons to thank for saving and donating the thousands of acres that became Acadia National Park, and for the miles of carriage trails and stone bridges that wind through it, giving unfettered access to hikers, and horses and cyclists. In my next life, if I don't come back as a cow, I'm coming back as a teacher, with several months of summer vacation.

JJ and I crossed the bridge to the island, and drove straight to a big cozy home on Somes Sound, full of folk art and artful folks who paint rocks and read Richelieu during breakfasts of lemon sponge cake and blueberry pancakes. The house is surrounded by great grassy meadows and of course… the dogs rolled around to cover themselves with the scent of Maine. They did this everywhere, but there was a special scent in the air evoking old memories, so they did synchronized wiggles in full concentric circles, fully absorbing the spirit of this place.

JJ stood up when we saw our hosts walking up the meadow pathway. They prepared to greet them with the same polite overly enthusiastic routine they have for everyone. But as the group drew closer, JJ's olfactory memory must have kicked in because they suddenly realized the familiar scent running towards us was… the *Puppy Nanny*! They were completely beside themselves. They twirled in circles and wriggled through and around her legs, rubbing and whimpering and covering her in kisses, collapsing into her lap—just like they were puppies once more. It had been five years since they'd seen her, and we'd arrived just in time to celebrate her 21st birthday.

We meandered along the mowed meadow path, past the raspberry patches and gardens of flowers and giant beanstalks and down to the tree house, where, on previous birthdays we had spent hours hanging candy from trees, so children could pick them whenever they please. We continued on past the dock to the *hammock grove*—where one could laze around listening to the plaintive calls of the loons, and gaze across the sound at a spectacular view of Cadillac Mountain.

They say that if you stand at the top of Cadillac Mountain in the early morning, the sun will touch you before it touches any other spot in the United States—and having been touched, you are inspired to climb every mountain, ford every stream, and sail off to explore every Blueberry, Cranberry and Porcupine Island in sight. And when you're done with all that, you can swim with the dogs in Sargent Mountain Pond and then gather in the garden of Jordan Pond House for baskets of hot popovers and proper cups of tea. This very civilized island tradition has been going on since 1847, and it's one that really ought to be adopted by other end-of-the-trail-destinations. I'm talking to you Pt. 16!

We headed back home for a quick game of croquet, which is never on the level and not at all cricket, but we weren't wearing hats so it didn't matter. And for dinner, we'd paddle canoes through phosphorescent waters across Somes Sound to the Lobster Pound. Or we'd stay home and gather around a Lazy Susan table laden with the usual Maine fare... lobster and butter, and corn and butter, and pasta and butter, bread and butter, and tomatoes and beans and butter... followed by a blueberry special, charades or poker, and maybe an evening walk around the meadow path—to round up anyone who might have fallen asleep down in the hammock grove.

And that's exactly what happened when we were touched by first sun on Cadillac Mountain.

Sunrise from Cadillac Mountain – Photo by: Jetson Jones CC SA 3.0

Maine to Michigan

It's a long way from Cadillac Mountain to Cadillac country, especially if one drives the back roads to go through Canada, which is the quickest route to the "UP"—Michigan's Upper Peninsula.

So JJ and I left the land of lobster rolls, fairy houses and fluffernut sandwiches and meandered west through Maine's farmland, marveling at the barn stars. Maine barns and houses are often a single unit, so in winter, farmers can run down the hall and milk the cows without ever having to leave home—which makes me wonder how cold it must get in Maine in winter.

Jenny and Jeff had been pouting since leaving their hiding place in the tall meadow grass on Somes Sound. They perked up when we stopped to hike through White and Green Mountains on our way to Canada via the Thousand Islands. This archipelago of 1,864 islands covers a 50-mile stretch of the St. Lawrence river, and is another one of those places the Gilded Age barons came to summer in the grand hotels, vacation homes and castles they had built on the islands.

And yes, these islands are the birthplace of Thousand Island dressing. Apparently the dressing began as a condiment a fishing guide's wife made for shore dinners. One patron loved it and got the recipe, and in turn gave it to the owner of Boldt Castle, which is on one of the islands. Boldt also happened to be the proprietor of the Waldorf-Astoria Hotel in New York. He put it on the menu there and the rest is history. For those of you who aren't familiar with it by that name, it is also the secret sauce used on In-and-Out burgers, and probably, Nepenthe burgers.

Our plan was to cross over the Thousand Island Bridge into Ontario, go up and around Georgian Bay to Sault St. Marie, and cross back over and down into Michigan. Then I discovered… my passport had expired. Ah, such a dilemma.

I was pretty sure I could get into Canada on an expired passport and driver's license, but could I get back to the US, and dare I chance it? As visions of authorities throwing JJ into the pound danced in my head, I stayed on the U.S. side of the border, turned left and headed for Toledo.

This is a very big country and there's a price to be paid to see it. There is never enough time in any one spot, and it takes a long time to get from one region to the next, with no time to stop at all the great places in between. So down, down, down we went in the sizzling heat through the Adirondacks, past wooden slatted armchairs, past Lake Placid, past the Thousand Islands to Niagara Falls.

As one drives along the Niagara River towards the falls, the flow turns to whitewater and the rapids become more violent. I was reminded of a scene from the Smithsonian Air and Space Museum's signature movie *To Fly*, where the balloonist calls down to the trapper paddling quietly along in a canoe to "get over… falls ahead." NO KIDDING. Apparently one fifth of all the fresh water in the world lies in four Great Lakes—Michigan, Huron, Superior and Erie. The outflow empties into the Niagara River and eventually cascades over Niagara Falls. So yes, these are indeed vast, amazing, humbling, awe-inspiring, breathtaking, overwhelming "falls ahead."

Niagara Falls

Log Cabins

Log Boathouses

Michigan's Upper Peninsula

We drove down around Lake Erie, past the Erie Canal and on through Cleveland, Toledo, and into the heart of Cadillac country. We barely stopped. We had to make up time we lost by not going through Canada. Finally we reached the Mackinac Bridge, the longest suspension bridge "between anchorages" in this hemisphere. We crossed onto the Michigan peninsula and up the road, under a canopy of maples until we arrived at the main gate to the camp.

I was somewhat surprised they let us in—very gypsyesque were we. Just five more miles along dirt roads, through primeval forests and across the wooden bridge to the shores of Lake Superior and the camp… another place from another time.

The camp was formed in the late 1800's as a fishing and hunting retreat, and ever since, generations of families have spent summers together here. It's a close-knit crowd. Fifty log cabins line Lake Superior's sandy beaches, and their log boathouses line the river that flows behind them. Wooden footbridges run across the river, connecting this slice of civilization with the wilderness beyond.

There is a general store and the lodge—its walls covered with old photos of blindfolded donkeys pulling building materials across the first wooden bridge; and photos of turn of the century ladies in full dress with corseted 18" waists rowing genteelly down the river, or gathering in groups for picnic dinners at one of the lakes; and of Aldo Leopold, a father of conservation, whose report on these mountains helped turn them into a site for research in field biology and geology.

We were greeted by gracious hosts, who politely ignored our disheveled appearance. Jenny and Jeff were given their own double dog bed to make them feel welcome, and I was given a collection of survival tools: a compass, forceps, a whistle, a cluster of bells and a rain jacket. I was loaded

JJ in Double Dog Bed

for bear should I get lost in a downpour and needed to pull porcupine quills out of the dogs' mouths and noses, and wanted to indicate my whereabouts by whistling out a proscribed number of blasts. Why do I need these things? Are they sending me into the wild alone? Are popovers and tea involved?

But I accepted these tools and instructions with grace… because those were the rules. This camp has many rules and traditions—unwritten rules that one was expected to know, such as dining room dress codes and where to sit; and ways to save places without looking like you're trying to create a "cool" table; and rules about leaving keys in the car so others could use it in case of an emergency; dropping your hat on the path to indicate you are fishing that hole—the elements of a culture passed from one generation to the next.

By day, we fished for cruising coasters and rainbow trout while JJ trolled for frogs; or we hiked the mountains and walked along crystal clear streams past rattlesnake orchids, wintergreen and wild sarsaparilla; and swam with the dogs in refreshing waterfall pools.

These people are naturalists one and all, and they certainly know their flora and fauna—and they know them all in Latin. We spotted deer and Sandhill Cranes and suffered no quills, though JJ's noses in the air and soft woofs strongly indicated that *something* was definitely out there. By night, we sat on our screened-in porch and mocked the giant flies, as the ancient call of the crane drifted over the lake. Then, we took to the boardwalk and gathered with friends for dinners at lodges and lake camps. And after that, we all sang songs... because those were the rules!

Hiking with JJ

Amber waves of grain

Sunflower fields

Michigan to Montana

Out of the Michigan woods and into the sunset in search of amber waves of grain. We headed west through Wisconsin's lush green valleys and wooded dells, and through Minnesota—land of 10,000 lakes. We rambled past expansive farms and neatly tended fields full of more corn—corn they needed to feed the dairy cows that produced all that creamy butter I had feasted on in Maine. Bread and butter go together—so where was the grain?

As we passed combines on the highway, I worried that all the crops had been harvested and I'd missed it—a hint that summer was waning and fall approaching. Then finally, finally… amber waves of grain! Field after field of grain— different shades of amber grain—oats, wheat, barley and rye fields folded into one another and then rolled into fields of sugar beets that rolled into great vast fields of bright yellow sunflowers.

It was so settled and peaceful there. It struck me as the one part of the country where things were not for sale—not the land, not the businesses or the well-kept houses with manicured lawns in small towns that dot the region—none of these were for sale.

All seemed to be well on the farm, so I turned my attention once again to our favorite traveling companion, Dr. Daniel Robinson, professor of philosophy and psychology at Georgetown and Oxford, who as you may remember, lectures me on the Great Ideas of Philosophy. This wasn't the first time I've heard these audiotapes, but I'd grown fond of Dr. Robinson's voice and marveled at his knowledge and use of language, so I listened again and again… and continued to hear new ideas and remember forgotten lessons.

As I passed North Dakota farms and grain fields, Dr. Robinson was talking about Faust, who as we all know, sold his soul to the devil in exchange for… for… what? Well, this apparently varies, but in Goethe's version, Faust is a tremendously learned fellow, who knows everything and is bored. So he trades his soul for an experience he would never tire of—an experience, which by its very nature would "cause him to ask time to stand still." So Faust goes through life and encounters great loves and grand passions and extraordinary experiences, but time marches on and still he is bored.

One day he is standing on a hill overlooking a farm, and he sees three people together in the fields happily working their own land. He finds this experience so rich, so extraordinary, so fulfilling, that he looks up to the heavens—and that's when he asks time to stop!

And that's when I started imagining what it would be like to live in North Dakota as a sunflower farmer working my own land and awakening to fields of bright, sunny petal-fringed sunflower faces every day. Then I thought about winter. And then I reached the Badlands.

The Badlands form a breathtaking, completely otherworldly landscape, and they must be very bad indeed because apparently only four consonants and two vowels

Badlands Evening – Photo by: Michael Kirch, CC BY SA 4.0

appear to have survived—as in the *Akta Lakota like Kadoka, Dakota a lot*. The rest of the letters were probably stolen by the Orphan Train refugees who ran off with Billy the Kid, and ended up hiding out in the Badlands. No one will ever find them, and they will never find their way out; destined to become a relic in one of the world's richest fossil beds.

JJ and I walked up a dry cracked mud pathway to look at the view. When we reached the ledge overlooking the vast strange terrain of eroded gullies and fanciful wall formations, we all gasped, jumped back and crouched down—completely intimidated by the landscape.

The Badlands have been described as surreal, the closest thing to a lunar landscape that can be found on Earth, a scenic marvel. Its ethereal pathways wind through chalk white, beige, rose and cream colored sculptured rock under a dazzling blue sky and blazing hot sun. There are no streams, no animals, no flowers or insects to bring life to the canyons, or keep you alive and hopeful should you get lost in the maze of eroded buttes, pinnacles, spires and lost vowels. And if you find yourself among the ruins at the bottom of the

canyon, you might find curious fossils of rhinoceroses, three-toed horses, camels, and ruminating hogs. The Badlands are eroding quickly and may only last for another 500,000 years, so if you plan to go… go soon!

Surrounding this arid moonscape, are vast grasslands once dense with bison—the life force of the nomadic Lakota Sioux who thrived there. In the late 1800's, the Country's westward expansion brought rough and ready fur trappers and mountain men, pioneers, homesteaders, bandits and gold seekers to the Black Hills. They took over the rich prairie lands for their farms and towns, and killed off all the buffalo—leaving the native people who had lived there for 10,000 years without sustenance. Skirmishes between the Lakota and the settlers and soldiers occurred with greater frequency—culminating in the horrifying Massacre at Wounded Knee.

Today, these vast grassy plains are teeming with buffalo once again, setting the scenes in *How the West Was Won*, *The Last Hunt*, *Bury My Heart at Wounded Knee*, *Dances with Wolves*, and countless other western classics.

Visions of Kevin Costner's horse Cisco and Two Socks the wolf danced in my head as we drove through Badlands National Park, until I noticed the motorcycle traffic and was jerked back into the 21st century. There were hundreds of cyclists, and it dawned on me that their numbers had been increasing since Wisconsin. I recalled hearing something about bikers gathering every year in South Dakota. So I left the Badlands labyrinth (thank heavens there was a road) and headed for Rapid City where I planned to "bed down" for the night as they say out here.

Rapid City was hopping with more motorcyclists—Hells Angels gangs as well as Yuppies and Bobos on Harleys. The two rooms that were left in town were going for $450 a night, so I kept going. Then I saw a sign for Sturgis—home of the

Sturgis Motorcycle Museum and Hall of Fame—and in an "ah ha" moment, realized that this was where the rumored annual gathering of 500,000 motorcyclists were all headed. And they were likely headed there from the west as well as the east, so there probably wouldn't be any reasonable places to stay for miles.

So we headed north to the Theodore Roosevelt Park, and finally stopped at a "guest ranch" overlooking even more grasslands. This was not some fancy tenderfoot ranch resort with horses and cowboys and hot springs, but rather a funky little motel that had tried to create a wild-west themed town with a saloon and casino, but didn't quite make it. However, it did have vast grassy views, and JJ could run right out the back door and off the deck and become part of them.

And so they did. Much to everyone's surprise, they ran right into a diabolical donkey and a horse that seemed to belong to no one. Jenny barked and trotted over to sniff the donkey, and the donkey sent her flying across the yard, where she landed with a whimper. The donkey turned to go after her, but Jeffrey moved in—distracting the donkey and giving Jenny time to hightail it back up to the deck. Jenny's hightailing distracted the donkey, so Jeffrey made a break for it, got back on the deck and we all scurried back to the room, where we attended to Jenny's skinned lip and bruised alpha ego. Meanwhile the donkey and his horse friend were not giving up. When I went out the door to the car, they had come around the backside of the building, and were sauntering down the *boardwalk* checking out every room… looking for us! Time to skedaddle and head for Big Sky Country.

Photo Courtesy of: Bill Mercer ReMax Mountain Property

"Fly fishing the blue ribbon Madison River near ThreeDollar Bridge in the beautiful Madison Valley."

Montana, The Last Best Place

We swept across the fruited plains into Montana—home to majestic purple mountains, big blue skies and sweeping green valleys. Montana is a stunningly beautiful state with a colorful past and an apt name. It has more mountain ranges per capita than all the other states combined—hence its name, which was derived from the Spanish *montaña* or mountain. What Montana lacks in imaginative etymology, it makes up for in nicknames—"Big Sky Country," "The Treasure State," "Land of the Shining Mountains," and "The Last Best Place."

We headed for Ennis in the heart of the Madison River Valley just outside of West Yellowstone. Anglers from around the world come to fish for trout in the blue ribbon waters of the Madison, Jefferson and Gallatin rivers that converge here. We drove into town expecting to see people in olive khaki shorts and fishing vests. But alas, it was "gun show weekend" and the street people were all in camouflage. It was enough to make me want to skedaddle again, but we headed for the river instead. JJ rolled happily in the grass, disguising their Upper Peninsula scent, and joined the ranks of the camouflaged. I just gazed at the scenery in awe, and wondered why everyone didn't move here and grow sunflowers.

Then the wind started to blow, bringing more wind and rain and snow. Yes… the first snow of the season… and it was only September for heaven's sake. The wind and cold put a damper on our fishing and hiking plans, but my hosts assured me that gambling was now legal in Montana, giving us new options for an evening out. We could cruise around looking for a hot table and then ride it… OR, we could go to an albacore feast to support Henry's Lake. On to the Lake we went.

Out here, where the waters are wide and fast flowing, the lakes are becoming an appealing alternative to rivers and streams, particularly for those who can't see rising fish as well as they once did. Seasoned fishermen now sit in boats on a quiet lake and listen for trout to gulp, and then cast in that direction. I wasn't aware that trout gulped… audibly… and I figured it was just another questionable fishing tale to add to the list. The list includes a story about how tickling a trout's stomach will make it stop wiggling so you can then catch it with your bare hands. Another is about the novice fly fisherman who caught a guppy on his first back cast, and then a big rainbow ate it. So he caught the rainbow—or was it a bird he caught on the back cast? Or did the bird eat the guppy? It's all a jumble, so I wasn't sure if I should believe the gulping trout tale.

The next day we left Montana, drove through Targhee Pass and stopped at Henry's Lake so JJ could romp and swim, and I could listen in silence for gulps. And then I heard it. I heard a trout gulp, looked over and saw a ripple. Then I heard another and another, and my imagination took over. And for a few brief shining moments, I was casting perfect loops straight toward the sound and bringing in huge cutthroat, brook and rainbows on a lake surrounded by snowcapped mountain peaks. At that moment, I thought Montana might just well be the "Last Best Place"—even though we were in Idaho!

We followed the Henry's Fork River through Idaho as it flowed into the Snake River and over Shoshone Falls. There we turned to head through the Nevada outback to the "Next Best Place"—Echo Lake, CA.

Madison Valley, Ennis, MT

Echo Lake – Photo by: Scorewith German, CC BY SA 3.0

California, Golden State

Echo Lake

I can only imagine how the pioneers must have felt after weeks of crossing Nevada's high desert past evaporating water mirages, dried out old bones, broken down wagons and *blown out tires*, and finally seeing the snow-capped Sierra Nevada mountains rise straight up from the desert floor—seducing weary travelers with their cool clear alpine lakes, grassy meadows, mossy pines, fir trees and… gambling casinos.

JJ were not of age, so we ignored the casinos and continued forth to Echo Lake, and back in time and memory to the summers of my youth. Echo Lake is one of many smaller glacial lakes in the "California Alps" as this part of the Sierra is known. It is blessedly undeveloped but for the small cabins built along its shores. The land is leased from the US Forest Service and there are no roads, so the only way to bring in the makings of a house is to take many trips by small boat. And so these homes remain rustic, cozy, authentic lake cabins… with huge stone fireplaces, lofts and wide porches with vast views and plenty of space for deck-sleeping with dogs.

When I started this trip, I mentioned a bucket list, which involved hiking every mountain and fording every stream from here to Maine and back. But that changed somewhere along the way—probably in Delaware and coastal Massachusetts where there are fewer high mountains and way too many streams. Since then, my goals were to train the dogs to stay behind me when I cast; ignore any fish I might catch; and go kayaking with me—in the boat.

At Echo Lake it happened. We did it. I knew that we could do it, and with the help of my hosts, indeed we did. It took three patient people, but we got JJ into the kayaks, gripped them with our knees and paddled into the horizon—

across the lower lake, through the "magical passage" and into the upper lake, where we enjoyed a celebratory picnic on the beach.

Needless to say, I now have visions of getting a sea-worthy kayak built for me and JJ so we could paddle in comfort from Big Sur to Baja and back, behind the whales, and then north to Alaska. Such a journey would certainly take a village, and I'm still looking for adventuresome villagers to accompany me.

Kayaking on Echo Lake – Photo by: Frank Graetch

Gold Country

JJ were reluctant to leave Echo Lake, a sentiment expressed from their latest hiding place under the porch. But we were in familiar territory and they knew we were heading for home, so they climbed into the car and assumed their positions.

When you're at the top of the mountain, all roads head downhill and eventually flow into Carmel—if that is your wish. We decided to continue our journey and wend our way through the foothills, through gold rush country to the towns around Angel's Camp, Sonora and to Yosemite. We would have loved to spend time in Yosemite, but alas, one of the many things I've learned on this trip is that national parks are not the best places for dogs. Seems they are only allowed on-leash in parking lots and that's about it. If I'd had any ideas about hiking through the valley with JJ under the shadow of Half Dome, they were quelled.

Instead, we meandered through the gold mining towns that Sunset Magazine invariably names among the best small towns in California—all of which are on my *potentially perfect polis* spreadsheet. These towns do have nearly everything—they are close to Yosemite and thus surrounded by natural scenic beauty; they have charming western movie set villages; there are plenty of mountain trails for off-leash dog walking and hikes; and they have independent bookstores, NPR stations and lots of festivals—music festivals, grape-stomping festivals, street fairs and car shows, and of course frog jumping festivals. They don't have a saint for a founding father, few towns do. But California's gold mining history is certainly alive and vibrant here, and I feel a distant connection to my 49er roots!

Yes, apparently I have a great-grandfather who was among the waves of immigrants who came west during the California Gold Rush, or so the story goes. I always imagined him to be a rough-and-tumble swashbuckling sort—braving the dangerous journey along the emigration trails from Pennsylvania to Missouri and on to California to stake out mining claims. One would think he must have been a dashing adventurer to move to California in the 1850's, and maybe he was. But the truth is, he came as an *accountant* to work for San Francisco Gas Company, a predecessor company of PGE. Somehow, coming west as an accountant during the gold rush doesn't seem terribly romantic—but very sensible and ever so Scottish. And it must be true because, why would anyone make up such a boring story!

There was so much more to see in the area, but summer travels were over and home beckoned. So we headed west toward the Salinas Valley, "Salad Bowl of the World." In Steinbeck's day, the major salad crop was lettuce… iceberg lettuce… though artichokes probably counted as a salad crop, since they really are their own complete salad course. Today the valley is equally known for its strawberries, spinach, tomatoes and vineyards—producing various grapes of wine and wrath.

As we meandered through the artichoke fields, JJ stuck their noses out the window sniffing, the salty ocean air. By the time we reached Carmel, they were standing at full attention, tails rotating like helicopter blades. My heart always catches when I turn onto Ocean Avenue and first see that clear blue Pacific water sparkling in the warmth of a perfect Indian Summer day. The water draws you to it. So we headed straight down Ocean Avenue, jumped out of the car, tumbled down the sand dunes into the waves, and raced along the beach in search of friends with cookies and fresh piles of kelp!

Home at last, and the time had come to wash the red dust and splattered bugs off the car, clean the dog hairs out of the computer keys, pack away the sleeping bags and fishing gear and cowboy boots, order a double dog bed, find a triple kayak, learn to draw and sing—and write the collection of thank-you notes that would become the essence of this tale.

JJ home on Carmel Beach – Photo by: Stefani Esta

To send a letter is a good way to go somewhere, without moving anything but your heart.
Phyllis Theroux

LORI STEWART is an award-winning author of multi-generational books. Born and raised in northern California, she graduated from Santa Clara University in economics and headed east to New York and Washington DC for careers in finance and technology. She ran AFTA Associates, a non-profit she founded to support wildlife conservation through community enterprise She returned to her California roots and now lives and writes in Carmel, and serves as an advisor to Ceca Foundation; and to the innovative *Read to Me Project*.

Layout & Cover Desing by: Chad B. Freeman
Cover Photo by: Philip Geiger, Carmel, CA

Photograph Credits
The photographs illustrating Travels with JJ are the work of the author unless otherwise noted in their captions. Permission to publish these illustrations has been graciously granted by the photographers, or were available under Creative Commons Attribution Share Alike licenses.

"Delicious. I learned so much and in such a gentle, enthusiastic way... history, geology, philosophy, fauna and flora not to mention the caprices of beloved dogs. I raced through it and was bereft when the travels were over."

ANNE GARRELS, award-winning journalist, long-time foreign correspondent for NPR, and critically-acclaimed author of *Naked in Bagdad*, and *Putin Country*. She lives on a farm in Norfolk, CT.

"Not everybody has two golden retrievers and a golden chance to drive across the country with them, connecting with old friends in beautiful places along the way. But in Travels with JJ you can do just that - sharing her adventures, listening to her stories and feeling as if you've had the best kind of an adventure with the best kind of guide. I'd follow Lori Stewart anywhere, on or off the page."

PHYLLIS THEROUX, essayist, columnist, teacher and critically acclaimed author of *The Journal Keeper, California and Other States of Grace* and other books. She lives in Ashland, VA

"There is no more delightful or eloquent travel companion than Lori Stewart. Tag along for this happy sojourn across our great country and back. You'll learn much from a lively narrator who loves dearly the natural wonders of this beautiful place we call home. It may even inspire you to hop in a car, find a pair of congenial golden retrievers for company and follow her trail. If so, Bon Voyage!"

MARGARET McGIRR, Greenwich, CT

In this charming, lighthearted account, Stewart writes about rescuing a litter of newborn orphan puppies—a project that began as an effort to engage her aging mother, and turned into soup for their souls. She raises two of the puppies, Jenny and Jeff (JJ) and travels with them across America, to visit old friends in fondly remembered places. They drive from California's sandy beaches to Maine's rocky shores and back, while listening to the "Great Ideas of Philosophy." Along the way, they explore the volcanoes and moss covered rainforests of the Pacific Northwest; the mountains and rivers, arid high-desert and wild-open spaces of the Mountain West; the Great Plains and Great Lakes of the Midwest; and the cities and farms and summer places of the Eastern Seaboard. They learn about the lifecycles of mayflies, lodgepole pines, horseshoe crabs, and kelp; and begin to understand the geology, regional history and cultural landscape of this vast, imperfect, and perfectly beautiful country.

$16.9
ISBN 978-0-9839293-2-
5169
9 780983 929321